REVEALING THE GREEN MAN

I much enjoyed this book. Mark Olly has done a grand job of research and the pulling together of many ancient tales and so revealing more of the nature of our ancient woodland guardian. Olly's style is very readable and draws you deeper and deeper into the book.

Reading *Revealing the Green Man* was an answer to one of those calls we all make when on a quest ourselves. I was looking for more about the Green King and then this book falls in my lap. It searches through our old stories and t ions into the unstoppable cycle of life, death and r   But Olly doesn't stop there, he brings in the g   minine, which is so important, the goddess a   gether. Indeed, he calls the book 'a danc   that's very well worthwhile joining in th
Elen Sentier, author of *Ele   , the Goddess* and *The Celtic Chakras*

For a small book, this text covers a s. ggering amount of ground, going far beyond the obvious foliate face to create an international insight into Green Men through history. With fascinating details from the past, startling connections and informed speculation, Mark Olly opens the door not just to rethinking Green Men, but to seeing humanity in new ways.
Nimue Brown, author of *Druidry and Meditation, Druidry and the Ancestors* and *Pagan Dreaming*

Reading through this book I kept thinking 'Aaah! Yes!' and musing to myself 'I'd never thought of it like that before' or remembering things I'd thought I'd forgotten as I travelled through this whistle-stop tour of ancient cultures. Mark Olly has managed to link together many of the masculine archetypes of the collective unconscious in his pursuit of the Green Man – with a few leaps of faith along the way – but it is a book I know I will enjoy reading even more the second time around.

Melusine Draco of the Coven of the Scales

This book is a love note to the male spirit of the green wood; the dying and resurrected god. Most aspects of the Green Man mythos are covered; from green metals (copper), green stones (jade) and copper painted blue/green Britons who attacked the invading Roman armies, to the dying and ever-living Christ.

While predominately British focused, the book makes brief forays into other cultures; the green deities of Nepal and Tibet, African fertility gods (and a brief mention of goddesses), South American jungle gods, the Islamic figure 'Al-Khidr' (the green one) and the Green Knight of Medieval legends. Robin Hood, Jack-in-the-Green and Herne the Hunter are discussed. The Jewish Tree of Life and the Scandinavian World Tree (Yggdrasil) make an appearance. The Victorian Holly King of Christmas card fame and the earthy characters of Tolkien and C.S. Lewis are mentioned. Witchcraft, Wicca and the modern New Age leafy faces of the Green Man are examined.

The book will be a satisfying read if you are interested in the male side of things. Another volume could easily be devoted to the Green Woman, to Mother Nature, to the Celtic, Scandinavian, Japanese and Egyptian understanding that the sun is female (not just male), and devotion paid to the fairies whose favorite color is green according to Celtic lore.

Ellen Evert Hopman, author of *A Legacy of Druids – Conversations with Druid leaders of Britain, the USA and Canada, Past and Present* and other volumes

Revealing the Green Man

The Restoration of the Oldest Religion
on Planet Earth

Revealing the Green Man

The Restoration of the Oldest Religion on Planet Earth

Mark Olly

MOON
BOOKS

Winchester, UK
Washington, USA

First published by Moon Books, 2016
Moon Books is an imprint of John Hunt Publishing Ltd., Laurel House, Station Approach,
Alresford, Hants, SO24 9JH, UK
office1@jhpbooks.net
www.johnhuntpublishing.com
www.moon-books.net

For distributor details and how to order please visit the 'Ordering' section on our website.

Text copyright: Mark Olly 2015

ISBN: 978 1 78099 336 2
Library of Congress Control Number: 2016935416

A CIP catalogue record for this book is available from the British Library.

Design: Stuart Davies

All internal photographs, graphics, and illustrations are by Mark Olly, along with specially
commissioned computer design images by digital artist Anthony Potts, unless otherwise stated.

Front cover image: 'The Woodland Master' by Anthony Potts

Printed and bound by CPI Group (UK) Ltd, Croydon, CR0 4YY, UK

We operate a distinctive and ethical publishing philosophy in all
areas of our business, from our global network of authors to
production and worldwide distribution.

CONTENTS

Dedicated to the memory of Margaret Ada Allcock (1932-2015).
'My doorway into this world – now returned to the green earth.'

Introduction and Terminology

Let not him who seeks cease until he finds, and when he finds he shall be astonished.
The Gospel of Thomas (C.100-110 AD)

The term 'Green Man' may be an invention of the twentieth century, but the creation behind it certainly is not.

Humankind has always stood in awe of things over which we have no control such as life and death, time, space, infinity, destiny, nature, and good old planet earth. In a strange way, while technology, exploration, science, and knowledge have all developed and increased, the basic lack of control over these 'immense' things has remained exactly the same today as it was far back in prehistory. It is from this inheritance that the Green Man rises like a vaguely remembered acquaintance we feel we should all know but, for some reason, we still view with fear and caution. There are some things over which we will never exert our control or, in some cases, never even fully understand. A 'cute and cuddly' chubby face peering at us through the leaves – I think not!

Using recent archaeological and historical discoveries, this book aims to reveal the real reasons behind the development and existence of the Green Man and what the symbol really represents to humankind – an almost lost dark religious thread running throughout time and still underpinning the very supports of our 'civilized' society. As magic is often referred to as 'The Golden Thread', so the Green Man sits behind even magic itself, exerting his very own 'golden' influence over it. He will be gradually revealed in this book to represent the very underlying magic of the earth itself.

This book is not intended to be a complete and final work in itself; there are far too few words here to completely do the subject matter justice. Rather it is intended as a pointer to further research. It is up to you, the reader, to explore, investigate, and most of all experience, that which constitutes the Green Man, underpinning nature wherever you may find him – or wherever he chooses to reveal himself, if you know what to look for. This is why there is no bibliography in this book and references have been credited as they appear and kept to a minimum. If you cast the net wide you will be amazed at how many connections you will make. It will be a revelation.

As far as terminology goes, the term 'Green Man' can be somewhat misleading. The term 'Foliate Head' is better, but still draws attention from many other physical and spiritual representations of the 'life force' that don't have foliage, frequently are not green, and very often not even human! Nevertheless they are all directly linked.

Such depictions can be found in the form of animals such as lions, tigers, bears, and many mythical beasts; in the form of human heads, faces and skulls, male, female, Jesus and the saints, other gods (possibly even the occasional 'Odin'), and sometimes, but rarely, goddesses – although the force being represented is almost always male.

The foliage or 'leaves' are also sometimes important to the meaning, such as oak, ash, elm, holly, grape vine, even flowering plants, corn, barley or tree roots, but frequently the foliage is just a design consideration, absent altogether, or replaced by other things.

Depictions span the full reach of time and geography. The impulse to depict this essential life force can be found way back in the mists of prehistory, from Middle Eastern and Far Eastern cultures before 4000 BC, in jungles and forests, mountains and rivers, and even deserts and wildernesses, where the desire to see the life force return was most likely the strongest of all.

The key was always balance, a contradiction when we note that almost all Green Men are just that – men! But these 'men' don't just live, they die, and it is this endless, unstoppable cycle of life, death, and hopefully resurrection, that the ancients mostly attributed to men.

Women have always been the other side of the scales, the representation of life, birth, fertility, and all things bright; that mysterious creature through which, and only through which, humankind and living things of all kinds, continue to appear. While the man may worship the woman for the entry of life into this realm, the woman may worship the man for life's departure to an after-life of some kind. As the 'warrior man' broadly represents the spiral down to death, the 'pregnant woman' represents the cycle of life and birth. It 'takes two to tango' the dance of life – and long will it remain so.

For the purposes of this book we will use the modern term 'Green Man' as defining the image and force about which we speak, and his story is long. I think you will find this book 'a dance', but I hope you will find the steps and the revelation that follows worth taking.

Mark Olly
Spring 2016

'The Ancientwood Lord' by Anthony Potts

1. Herne and Horns

If God did not exist, it would be necessary to invent him.
Voltaire (1694-1778)

It's winter around 30,000 BC and the snow and ice lie in a thick, white blanket across the land, providing a stark reminder of the former Ice Ages through which humankind has been forced to survive. Inside a dry, fire-lit cave a huddled group of skin-clad hunters gaze on as one of their number dances dressed in the hide and antlers of a large deer, casting ever-twisting grotesque shadows across walls painted with hunting scenes and signed with hand prints from many ages past.

We know this story to be true because we still have European cave paintings that show these hunters dressed in animal skins and horns at Trois-Frères, in Ariege, France, and the surviving antler head pieces from Starr Carr, South Yorkshire, England. In times when survival was undoubtedly of the highest priority, what were these people trying to achieve by indulging themselves in performing arts?

What we do know is that a great deal of time and effort was put into recording hunting scenes on cave walls after the last Ice Age had all but ended, and that dressing up in the ways shown in these paintings would be very poor camouflage for hunting, especially considering a deer's ability to smell a hunter's scent and recognise the silhouette of a standing human figure at a distance!

What we do have is probably the first representation of the Shaman of the Hunt undertaking a ceremony, probably for one of two reasons. Firstly this was possibly in thanks for a good season's hunting and to honour the deer that died to provide food or, secondly, quite the opposite, possibly a magical act to try to attract the much-needed herds that, for some reason, had failed to appear at the appointed time.

This last option would appear the favourite considering the high priority of survival.

Either option being the case we have the first physical indications of a belief that humankind could somehow influence the natural world around them through a complex form of sympathetic magic presumably used at the appropriate times of the year. We also have here the very root birth of the figure much later known as Herne the Hunter, the first and oldest lord of the forest to be historically recorded by early Europeans.

Also implicit in the belief is the connection between the human (shaman), the object (antlers), and the desired aim in the natural world (deer), conveyed by some other inherent force which must inevitably flow through all things. Then the Stone Age came to an end and the Copper Age and Bronze Age began.

The two sets of 'shaman's horns' unearthed at Starr Carr post-glacial cave systems in South Yorkshire taken from 19th century archaeology reports

The Solar Copper Cult Begins

6000 BC – Copper smelted in Anatolia and the Caucasus; the Gilgamesh Epic composed.

4500 BC – Smelting takes place in the Balkans, Mediterranean and Central Europe.

3350 BC – Earliest date for Otzi the Iceman and his copper axe (3100 BC at latest).

3000 BC – Egyptians worship the 'Aten' (Sun), Osiris and the fertility of the Nile.

2000 BC – Copper is mined on the Great Orme, Llandudno, Wales, UK.

1950 BC – Copper is mined on Alderley Edge, Cheshire, England, UK.

'The Huntsman Gazes Upon Standing Stones' by Anthony Potts

2. The Watchman of the Forest Never Sleeps

The first written account to survive of a 'force' found in the vast forests uncharted and unaffected by man is The Forest Journey in the Middle Eastern Babylonian pre-flood tale known as *The Epic of Gilgamesh*, which was miraculously preserved on clay tablets found in desert ruins by early archaeologists and first translated in the 19th century. The *Epic* is at least between 5,000 and 6,000 years old, takes us back into the mind of Bronze Age man, and points mysteriously to the traditions of beheading and the 'triple death' found in European Celtic sacrifice.

Various dates have been given to planetary floods between 10500 BC and 3500 BC and it has to be accepted that there must have been many minor regional floods at the end of the last Ice Age and at least one big one, which probably led to the Biblical flood account, the Egyptian-Greek 'sinking of Atlantis', and many more including the Babylonian's own *Epic* version of a super-flood found in the clay tablets – but this is not the subject of our quest here. It merely serves to draw a line fixing the date of our tale in a world as yet unravaged by the waters of melting ice or the wholescale human environmental deforestation of the recent ages. In the story, the hero Gilgamesh meets the eyes of his companion Enkidu and says:

'Because of the evil that is in the land, we will go to the forest and destroy the evil; for in the forest lives Humbaba whose name is 'Hugeness', a ferocious giant.'

But Enkidu sighed bitterly and said, 'When I went with the wild beasts ranging through the wilderness I discovered the forest; its length is ten thousand leagues in every direction. Enli has appointed Humbaba to guard it and armed him in sevenfold terrors, terrible to all flesh is Humbaba. When he roars it is like the torrent of the storm, his breath is like fire, and his jaws are death itself. He guards the cedars so well that when the wild heifer stirs in the forest, though she is sixty leagues distant, he hears her. What man would willingly walk into that country and explore its depths? I tell you, weakness overpowers whoever goes near it: it is not an equal struggle when one fights Humbaba; he is a great warrior, a battering ram, Gilgamesh, the watchman of the forest never sleeps.'

Here we have a perfect description of the wind roaring in the trees, the mystical movement of the canopy, the peculiar way sound travels in a silent forest, that feeling of always being watched, no line of sight to tell of what lies hidden, the habitation of wild beasts and legendary creatures. The tale then unfolds that the giant (or 'huge') force of the forest must be executed before any cedar trees can be taken away for building purposes or the forest cleared. Evidently the *Epic* contains the memory of the first woodland clearances and the start of the change in attitude towards the 'sacred' woodland. Eventually Gilgamesh and Enkidu slay the giant Humbaba, but the gods are not pleased.

Gilgamesh listened to the word of his companions, he took the axe in his hand, he drew the sword from his belt and he struck Humbaba with a thrust of the sword to the neck, and Enkidu his comrade struck the second blow. At the third blow Humbaba fell. Then there followed confusion for this was the guardian of the forest whom they had felled to the ground.

At this point they set about clearing the forest then:

They set Humbaba before the gods, before Enlil; they kissed the ground and dropped the shroud and set the head before him. When he saw the head of Humbaba, Enlil raged at them. 'Why did you do this thing? From henceforth may the fire be on your faces, may it eat the bread that you eat, may it drink where you drink.' Then Enlil took again the blaze and the seven splendours that had been Humbaba's: he gave the first to the river, and he gave to the lion, to the stones of execration, to the mountain and to the dreaded daughter of the Queen of Hell.

Penguin Classics, translation 1972 by N. K. Sandars

Contained in this tale we have execution in three ways using a bronze sword and axe, which leads to beheading of a victim (possibly the biggest tree – Humbaba) whose head is then presented to the god. In turn the god distributes light and powers ('blaze' and 'splendours') to the natural world still remaining around them, the river, the open space where the lion now lives, the place of the sacred stones, the mountain, and the place of death and burial ('Hell').

Bog bodies are found in peat, peat forms from vast amounts of forest material, forests that are usually not there any more. In literary terms we are seeing here the recording of the first relevant myth at the onset of the forest clearance phase of human agriculture when humankind ceased to be hunter gatherers and became farmers. As time progresses in this part of the Middle East the Mesopotamian god-deity Tammuz may also contain aspects attributed to the Green Man as he is thought to symbolise the triumph of life over the hardships of winter. In Babylonia and Mesopotamia we also first encounter distinctive depictions of the Tree of Life, which may ultimately relate in some way to the previous story and may have lent its identity to the one found in later Jewish mysticism.

The sun also plays a part in the wisdom of these times, specifically relating to the very existence of the life-force and as the signal for another day of life on planet earth, which should always be used wisely:

Listen to the exhortation of the dawn!
Look to this day for it is life,
The very life of life!
In its brief course lie all the verities
And all the realities
Of your existence;
The bliss of growth,
The glory of action,
The splendour of beauty;
For yesterday is but a dream
And tomorrow is only a vision;
But today well lived
Makes every yesterday
A dream of happiness
And every tomorrow
A vision of hope.
Look well, therefore, to this day!
Such is the salutation of the dawn.
Attributed to Kalidasa and translated from Sanskrit, C.2500 BC

'Spirit of the Trees' by Anthony Potts

3. The Man in the Ice and the Man in the Chalk

The operations of the mind no doubt find their noblest expression in the language of speech, yet they are also eloquent in the achievements of the hand. The works on man's hands are his embodiment of thought, they endure after his bodily framework has passed into decay, and thus throw a welcome light on the earliest stages of his unwritten history.
Professor William Johnson Sollas (born 1849, died 1936) 'Ancient Hunters'

As stone technology gradually gave way to metal, the hunter societies of Europe settled into areas that archaeology can clearly identify as separate cultures. One such culture is that of the Alpine regions of central Europe, countries like Italy and Austria.

On Thursday 19th September 1991 two hikers from Nuremburg, Germany, were walking in the Otztal Alps when they came across a body sticking out of an ice sheet in the Tisenjoch area. Little did they know that they had come face to face with the last surviving complete body of a European prehistoric hunter.

Eventually the body was taken to a specially constructed deep-freeze storage facility at the South Tyrol Museum of Archaeology in Bolzano where it was carbon dated to everyone's amazement between 3350 BC and 3100 BC. Here also all the items subsequently found on and surrounding the body were

14

identified and reconstructed.

The assemblage clearly shows a master survivalist, hunter-gatherer and, possibly at the end of his life, a warrior with a stone arrow head embedded in his right shoulder and defensive knife wound cut across his right hand. He was given the name Otzi and of particular interest to us are his axe and tattoos.

His axe is one of a tiny few complete intact examples of prehistoric copper axes in the world and it immediately pushed the Bronze Age further back than previously thought by more than a thousand years. This has now given us a new time period – the Copper Age. At some point between 4500 BC and 3500 BC European humans had clearly discovered how to mine and melt bronze from the solid rock wherever it appeared in their territories.

From a practical point of view the copper axe could cut down soft-wood trees and act as first defence if attacked, but it was no substitute for the well-established stone equivalents at this point. Copper had a more symbolic meaning as 'the metal of the sun' and as a status symbol of the very latest human technology. Some things never change!

For a society that mostly thought in pictures and symbolism, without the clutter of letters and numbers, the formula must have gone something like this:

The damp earth turns green when the sun is hot – copper comes from the earth and is green when found and mined – once melted copper turns gold – the sun is gold and glows like the opening in a crucible – therefore copper comes from the sun – and so do green plants.

There is also a much darker formula we can apply to copper:

Copper is the blood of the earth – when melted it oxidizes and turns red – blood tastes very much like copper on the tongue – copper weapons cut and release blood – weapons are the property of warriors – warriors rule over life and death.

But where does the discovery of Otzi sit with prehistoric magic? The skills of the shaman had developed greatly since the end of the Ice Ages and the men of the painted caves. The ice man's body is covered in more than 50 precise tattoos that are exclusively rectangular carbon-black blocks arranged in groups over joints, which examination has shown would have given him pain – blocks except for two. On the inside of his right knee and beside his left Achilles tendon on his ankle he has an equal-armed cross.

From this period of history onwards this type of cross can be found all over the world, sometimes enclosed in a circle and frequently associated with the sun. This is the first and so far only time that human remains have been found with a clear and direct personal depiction of a cross on the body combined with the obvious possession of a largely ceremonial copper axe. It may also represent the earliest beginnings of acupuncture, which connects directly to the 'life force' so loved in Chinese medicine. Magic, life, copper, cross, the sun, all aspects we find very much connected from this point on.

The Copper Age slowly grew into the Bronze Age through a process that spread over most of Europe and the eventual discovery that tin, and some other metals, hardened copper into bronze. This is possibly best represented in Britain in recent times with the discovery and excavation of the Amesbury Archer on Friday 3rd May 2002 during construction of a housing estate and school in Amesbury Village, Wiltshire, England, about three miles from Stonehenge.

This male individual, one of several, was buried with the largest number of artefacts yet found in a Bronze Age grave in

Britain. Carbon dating places the date of burial to around 2400 BC to 2200 BC and five beakers found in the grave identify him as part of the Early Bronze Age 'Beaker People' who appear in Britain at this time from across the English Channel. Most important to our voyage of discovery is the presence in the grave of three tiny copper knives and a portable 'cushion stone' anvil indicating that he was most probably a coppersmith by trade. Further oxygen isotope analysis of his tooth enamel suggests he journeyed from the Alpine regions of Central Europe. The technology of the European Copper and Bronze Age had arrived on British shores.

As a parting observation to this period in history, one unique British example of an equal-arm cross from Southworth Hall, Lancashire, England, dating to around 1440 BC can be found incised into the base of an Early Bronze Age cremation burial 'cup' with clearly mathematical internal lines; one, then two, then three, possibly representing the best known formula for British Bronze at this time – one part tin/lead/zinc (17%) to two parts nickel/bismuth (31%) to three parts copper (52%). All of these elements are known to exist and be mined in the British Isles. Zigzag lines incised into the sides of such cups and urns are sometimes interpreted to represent 'water' to show that the person cremated inside had been a trader by river or sea. Equal-arm crosses on the base of urns of this and later periods in the British Isles are relatively common.

Once discovered, copper mines (and mines for other metals) flourished in areas with appropriate geology all across Europe, indeed the world. In Britain possibly our finest and oldest examples can be found at the Great Orme, Llandudno, North Wales, and at Alderley Edge Country Park, Alderley Edge, Cheshire, both of which can be said with reasonable confidence to date back to beyond 2000 BC. Unique carved bone fragments have been found in mines and caves on the Great Orme, stained green from the copper deposits, and there was once a circular arrangement of flowers and a cat skeleton in the main body of the mine interpreted as a prehistoric offering made by the miners, but this has unfortunately been destroyed by flooding.

Copper mined from all parts of the world retains its unique 'finger print' in its chemical composition. Copper from Britain has been found as far afield as ancient Egypt, and metals from Egypt have also been discovered on the European continent (such as Iron ingots showing phaoronic marks in Germany). Archaeological finds have clearly established that countries all around the Mediterranean (and possibly the Atlantic) were connected by sea trade during the Bronze Age and later Iron Age, no doubt also widely dispersing other human developments such as religion.

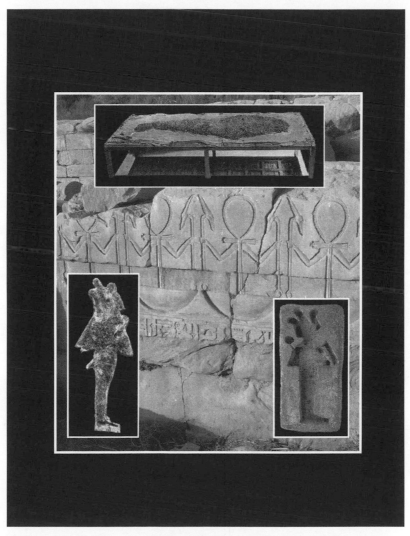

Osiris bed, Osiris mud cutter, and Osiris brick from 19th century
archaeology reports against a background of carved Ankh crosses
(Temple of Sekhmet, Karnak)

4. Egypt – A Matter of Life and Death

The nature of God is a circle, of which the circle is everywhere and the circumference is nowhere.
Traditional Proverb

After the last Ice Age the prehistoric world slowly gave rise to the familiar geography of today. The ice sheets retreated further north and lands closer to the equator became hot deserts. Such was the fate of Egypt.

We know that the flint tools, stone burial chambers, rock carvings, and other signs of prehistoric human activity can be found all over the world and, although not often indicated to the public, Egypt is certainly no exception. It was never the isolated desert backwater culture that antiquarians once imagined, in fact trade was taking place all around the Mediterranean from very early times producing a clear connection between 'Celtic' Europe and North African cultures such as Egypt. Early rock glyphs of boats and crosses found in Prehistoric Germanic and Scandinavian countries find an uncanny echo in the desert rock glyphs of Egypt.

Indeed the Fayum Oasis, in Egypt, has given up a perfectly preserved Celtic warrior's shield, and clay figurines of Celtic warrior mercenaries have also been found dating back to the third century BC. Celtic mercenaries are known to have been used by the Egyptians at various periods in their history stretching back some considerable time. In a startling twist, recent DNA analysis of royal mummies of the Armarna Period (New Kingdom, 18th Dynasty, 1552 BC to 1306 BC) has produced links back to Europe and the British Isles – even in pharaohs. The mummies of Amenhotep III, Akhenaten (formerly Amenhotep IV), and Tutankhamun have produced DNA that indicates an above 70% affinity with European men, and an above 94% probability that their lineage has British origins (where Swiss scientists

Nile Deity making offerings at the Temple of Rameses, Abydos

concluded that the highest concentration of their detailed ancient DNA group can now be found). It is thought that Akhenaten's daughter Meritaten fled to Britain following the fall of her father's dynasty, arrived in Southern Ireland to become the tribal leader 'Scotia' (founder of the Scots) and lies buried there still. For the family to be British/Celtic in origin it implies that mercenaries arrived much earlier in the 18th Dynasty, possibly before the time of Amenhotep III around 1400 BC. Not surprisingly then we find an abundance of various Green Men in Egypt from as early as 1300 BC.

At the most basic level we find a number of green painted human figures among hieroglyphs. Broadly speaking these represent fertility and are often making fertility offerings at temples, like those found at the Temple of Rameses at Abydos. Pharaohs like Rameses II are also sometimes shown painted green depending on the context of the depiction.

The god of the Nile is also often shown in green and blue and, at a higher level, we frequently find the old creator-god and patron of artists Ptah, whose name means 'modeller of the world', shown as a green-skinned figure, as in the tomb of Horemheb in the Valley of the Kings and in the tomb of Amon-her-khopsef in the Valley of the Queens.

Then moving to the highest level of the Egyptian pantheon we also frequently find Osiris, ruler of the underworld (the realms below ground), shown in shades of green and blue to represent fertility, re-birth and resurrection. The ultimate out-working of this principle can be shown in three surviving objects.

The first is an effigy of Osiris found wrapped in linen windings in a box in the Treasury of Tutankhamen in the Valley of the Kings which, when unwrapped, proved to be a frame filled with fertile Nile mud that had sprouted to produce a 'Green Osiris' or 'Corn Mummy'.

The second is a more permanent fired clay brick having a central Osiris-shaped chamber intended to be filled with the same mud and grain seeds as an offering at funerals. This too would sprout and produce a 'Green Osiris' rather like cress seeds do if placed in a window space on a bed of wet cotton wool.

Finally the third object is a full size 'Osiris bed' found in the tomb of Maihirpre, an Egyptian nobleman of the fourth century BC, which consists of a bed frame spread with a linen sheet on which rests the outline figure of Osiris drawn in silhouette in corn that has been left to germinate. It is known that, in one of his roles, Osiris is regarded as a corn-deity with the sprouting corn implying the similar resurrection of the deceased by the lifepower of Osiris. This is possibly the origin of the Corn Man, Corn King and John Barley Corn depictions found in Medieval Europe after the Crusades.

How manifold are all thy works! They are hidden from before us. O though sole God, whose powers no other possesseth. Thou didst create the earth according to thy desire. While thou wast alone: Men, all cattle large and small, All that are upon the earth, That go upon their feet; All that are on high, That fly with their wings. Akhenaten's 'Hymn to the Aten' (compare Moses Psalm 104 verses 20 & 21)

It will not have escaped the casual observer of all things Egyptian that the hieroglyph for the sun is a circle, and the equal-armed cross, often in a circle, appears prominently in Egyptian iconography throughout the BC period. In fact this is

the first society in which we find the symbol widely used in the form later adopted by the Coptic and Celtic Churches, the Knights Templar, and other orders with

Coptic cross at the entrance to the inner sanctuary, Temple of Isis, Philae

23

connections to the Middle East and North Africa.

Linguistically the pictogram 'line of the horizon' (earth) or that of 'bread' (loaf) is combined with the circle of the 'full sun' (Eye of Horus) and the vertical pole or 'backbone of Osiris' (Djed pillar) raised to point at the pole star Sirius during the spring Djed festival, similar in concept to our May Day festivities. The same three elements (vertical line, horizontal line, full circle) are combined differently in the long traditional 'Ankh' cross or 'Key of Heaven' and the Egyptian religious symbol of eternal life and the life to come beyond death.

The sun disc representing Egypt's supreme deity Ra (the 'Aten') was the element removed from the original cross when the sun worship element was dropped from the Christian religion to form the Christian cross known today. The beginnings of this may have happened as long as 1350 BC, before the birth of

Yeshua (Jesus), when Hebrews fleeing Egypt in the Old Testament turned to monotheism, began to worship a single unseen God, left sun worship behind, and made for the Promised Land under Moses.

This even speaks to an earlier time when written language was first developing from the only two possible basic elements; the dot (or circle) and the line. Alphabetically it has been shown that Egyptian developed into Protosinaitic, then Phoenician, which traders spread across the world where it became Early then Later Greek, and finally Latin. The Egyptian eye became O and the cross became T.

As far as the sacrifice of human beings for the salvation of humankind, few would argue that the cross has now become the ultimate symbol, although its intention nowadays is to demonstrate how Yeshua (Jesus) is the last and final human sacrifice.

'Hearn the Huntsman' by Anthony Potts

5. Beyond Dark Waters

Returning to Alderley Edge Country Park, Alderley Edge, Cheshire, England, and the green copper ore mined from the soft brown sandstone of Cheshire; it is known from the remains of open cast surface mines, stone mining hammers, and other processing tools in stone and wood, that mining has been taking place here since at least 1950 BC. A wooden 'trowel' found in the mines during excavations in 1875 and known as the 'Brynlow Shovel' was carbon dated by the Manchester Museum in May 1993 to 1888-1677 BC (calibrated) when it was recovered from a local junior school cupboard and handed in by world famous author Alan Garner who first saw it there as a child.

Alan lives in the shadow of Alderley Edge and also remembers the finding of two small Middle Bronze Age copper alloy axe heads (or 'palstaves') buried by the stream that flows

A typical selection of Bronze Age European offerings of copper and gold, many of them circular to represent the sun

directly from the Edge into Lindow Moss, one in a garden and another at the side of the brook. These offerings are not unique. All over the British Isles and Europe the Celts deposited millions of objects into earth and water to 'send them on to the next world' and many of those that have survived are made from metal, mostly iron, copper and gold, and there are some patterns we can discern.

Weapons such as swords, sword chains, axes, spears, knives, helmets, shields, and chariot parts are common, with other more random artefacts such as torque bracelets and neck rings, slave chains, hanging bowls, cauldrons, buckets, a sheet bronze calendar, broaches, clothing pins, bells, a bronze bed on wheels, chalices, mirrors, wine jugs, and some more obvious figures of animals, gods and goddesses, were all included as offerings in deposits and burials. The same range of goods must have also included wood, textiles, animal skin and leather, most of which have perished except for a few isolated examples from water-logged deposits, and of course some rare actual human remains.

What all this tells us is that a 'good sacrifice' had to be something of value, most frequently with a use that could in some way be regarded as sacred and connected to life and death, often deliberately damaged or destroyed (ritually 'killed'), of great value, and very often circular in shape to represent the sun. While the Celts practised the almost universally held belief that items could be buried with the significant dead in order to send them to the next life with them, they also had other ways of utilising dark waters such as rivers, streams, lakes and bogs to send things over to 'the other side'. This practice is also certainly not limited to Celtic Europe – it is almost a worldwide phenomenon with pretty much the same formula applied wherever it occurs.

Celts also had a distinctive art style, which included many natural plant and animal forms and foliate faces disguised in the swirling plant-like patterns and knot-work. They also went to great lengths in sculpting animals such as horses, wild boar, bears, cats, birds, fish, bulls, deer, and legendary creatures in many different materials including bronze, a practice that survived through and beyond Saxon times.

As a cautionary note – up to this point in history it was never assumed that anyone or anything ever came back in the same form from the 'underworld' or 'otherworld' once it had died. The concept of 'reincarnation' or a heaven in the skies simply did not exist. Souls could remain trapped in this world, pass over, or come back in some form exactly as the person who had departed (known as 'resurrection'), money and items could even be loaned in this life to be repaid in the next, but nothing was ever thought to be recycled or considered to exist 'up in the sky'. These are both much later concepts. In death the earth was king.

Wandering through the sunlit leafy mounds and ancient trees of Alderley Edge Country Park on an autumn day, with its huge collection of myths and legends, it's not hard to imagine the wonder early metal workers and miners must have felt at the magic of their art. Somewhere, sometime, someone must have built a fire on a stone prominence and noticed, when the embers died and the ashes scattered or washed away, tiny globules of something shiny and gold. Or possibly the green stone had turned red as the earth bled metal.

Maybe these folks scratched out the green powder from the now heat-fragmented sandstone rock and tried the process again with the same results. Possibly someone noted that ancient seasonal formula of greenery coming from the golden sun – and now they had reversed the process and brought forth gold from the green earth. The red blood in which resides the life of men could be taken hard from the earth to form a sacred golden metal – red, gold and green.

The copper smelting process evidently became sacred at a time in prehistory when ancient religion was changing and developing again and, just three miles north-west in the dark pools and peat bogs of Lindow Moss, the next step was about to reveal itself in graphic detail.

On the 1st August 1984 a worker on a peat extraction machine

at Lindow Moss, Wilmslow, Cheshire, England, picked up an obstruction from the conveyor belt heading for the shredder. Thinking it was a piece of wood he threw it aside and, when it hit the ground, the peat fell away to reveal a human foot!

Four months earlier the same workers, Andy Mould and Stephen Dooley, had found a human skull, which had turned out to be Iron Age (early British Roman Period), so the find was reported to the British Museum, the rest of the body located, and 'Lindow Man', or 'Pete Marsh/Pete Bog' was lifted from his watery peat encased grave some 2m (6ft) below the modern ground surface.

As probably the most famous of the four hundred or so complete or partial bog body finds across the British Isles and Ireland, little more needs to be said of the specific details of

Lindow Man – except for one crucially important and under reported analysis made in 1991 announced to the world at a seminar held in Cardiff in January 1992 and given as follows:

The opening story makes it clear that there were more than one set of human remains found on Lindow Moss:

A]. Body parts known as 'Lindow II' (1st August 1984) and 'Lindow IV' (12th September 1987) are the internationally famous upper torso, buttocks and leg of Lindow Man.

B]. Body parts known as 'Lindow I' (13th May 1983) and 'Lindow III' (6th February 1987) proved to be another individual, the skull and the rest of the body recovered in over 70 pieces, another adult male around 5ft 5ins tall with a grossly malformed thumb on his right hand.

Lindow Man photographed on a visit to the Manchester Museum during filming for an ITV television series

The Cardiff seminar reported on a detailed skin search of both sets of human remains (initially to establish if either man had tattoos) and concluded that:

> *There is exciting evidence of this body (Lindow I & III) being painted with a bright blue clay-based copper paint. This is not the woad of schoolbook translations of Caesar, which does not appear in the archaeological record until the Saxon period. However, here at last is evidence for the blue-painted naked Celtic warriors that struck such awe into the Roan soldiers. Subsequent re-examination of Lindow Man (Lindow II & IV) shows the same group of chemicals in his skin.*

The article continues:

> *Oxford and Harwell, have produced complementary dates which, when calibrated, give a range AD25-230 with 95% confidence limits: i.e. the first half of the Roman occupation of Britain.*
> Cheshire Past Issue 2, Page 10, The Lindow Moss Bog Bodies: Further Research by Rick Turner, CADW

This report proves a vital key and pivotal turning point in our search for the real Green Man. There is no doubt that both the Lindow men were human sacrifices sent on their way to the Celtic 'otherworld' below the dark mirror waters of the moss lands, misty forest doorways to the next world but, most crucially, they were sent there painted blue-green with the copper from the nearby copper mines. Ritually 'killed' in three ways (strangled, stabbed, drowned) their green faces would have slowly sunk into the black water as floating leaves fallen from nearby trees swirled around them giving birth to the image of the first Green Men in all their true meaning and glory.

Not only did they represent the ancient British culture that, at that time, was taking a hammering from the invading Romans who had defeated the combined Celtic tribes and overrun Anglesey, but they also departed wearing the 'skin of the sun', which would assure them an audience with the highest gods if not the very giver of life. The initially refined and powdered copper from which their ritual coating was made may even have started as a shining gold 'glitter paint', which oxidized in contact with skin and sweat to quite literally dye the skin dark green before their very eyes.

History tells us that the Romans ultimately assimilated the British Isles into their empire, but also became the next step in the relentless development of the solar copper cult. Some researchers have seen parallels between the Celtic sun god Lud, also known as Nodens, and the Green Man, but evidence appears to indicate that the realm of the Green Man's force clearly lay here on earth, if not even down below in the earth itself.

Stand in a silent and ancient wood, or on the banks of a still dark pool, close your eyes, and try to be aware of the life teeming around you. It's not just jungles like the Amazon that contain vast quantities of life. All woodlands have life living upon life; even the soil, the rocks and the trees all contain life. Here is the 'force' of the Green Man. Deep, alive, ever-present in sight, smell, sound, even taste. Hot as the sun on your face, wet as the brown peaty water seeping between your toes, alive as the breeze that rustles the leaves.

You are doing exactly the same thing that the Celts and other humans would have done thousands of years ago, listening to the same sounds and connecting with the same life. Perhaps the difference for us today is that we can generally feel safe. In the woods back then lived animals that could do serious and permanent harm and all nature deserved the utmost and absolute respect. Feel the warm sun once again as it shines through the leafy canopy – and it is time to move on again.

Bronze Age copper mine on Alderley Edge in Cheshire

In a more up-to-date discovery at Alderley Edge a broken pot containing bronze Roman coins dating to 330 AD to 340 AD was recovered by the Derbyshire Caving Club, buried in the top of a deep 13m (40ft) vertical sandstone shaft, which also proved to be Roman. Possibly this represents Roman use of Alderley copper for coins, later buried as an offering when this particular shaft was ritually closed down. The face of the Roman Emperor, after all, was the face of a god!

Harvest and fertility figures from the corners of a well preserved Roman mosaic in Tunisia

6. The Face of the God – We Came, We Saw, We Went Home Again

The eye of the great god, The eye of the god of glory, The eye of the king of hosts, The eye of the king of life, Shining upon us through time and tide, Shining upon us gently and without stint. Glory be to thee, O splendid sun, Glory be to thee O sun, face of the god of life.

Ancient Celtic Hymn to the Sun, Translation by Barry Fell in the book *America B.C.*

Turning our attention to the other side of the coin concerning the invasion of Celtic Britain; Julius Caesar states in his *Gallic Wars* that it was believed that the institution of Druidism had originated in Britain and that many still went there in order to acquire a more perfect knowledge of the system. Caesar also records that, on an appointed day in the year, a general assembly of Druids would be held in the territory of the Carnutes *'in the centre of all Gaul'* – not just the geographic centre, but also the spiritual. Here they held sessions on a consecrated site. Caesar says: *'Hither, those who have disputes bring them from all parts and submit them to the Druids for arbitration.'* The geographic centre of Druidic Britain would indeed have been somewhere in the north west of the country, perhaps not too far from Lindow Moss. Then we have the famous account of what happened when Julius Caesar first arrived here.

On the 5th August 55 BC, Julius Caesar, the greatest Roman military general of all time, crossed the English Channel from Witsand near Calais with two already terrified divisions of Roman troops.

Fifty-five days later this finest of international fighting forces, which had defeated the best armies in Europe and Asia at this time, had moved no further than seven miles from its landing point. Essentially beaten and very upset, Caesar retreated back to the continent with the intention of 'giving it another go' the following year.

On the 10th May 54 BC he was back with five legions of Rome's best fighting men, possibly as many as 60,000 troops, and a fleet of a thousand ships. Dion Cassius records that he was intending to take the fight to the interior of Britain, but still found his forces inadequate to face the opposition thrown at him by the Celtic British under Caswallon.

Nevertheless Caesar soldiered on for four months, but penetrated only seventy miles in-land with his main force pinned down on the Kent coast by Celtic forces.

On the 10th September 54 BC he concluded a hasty and undoubtedly humiliating peace at St Albans and sailed back to France under the cover of darkness. It was almost a hundred years and the times of Lindow Man before Roman eyes were to look across the Channel towards Britain again. Only Caesar's rhetoric lived on in the form of the often quoted, but vitally important comment:

Most of the inland inhabitants do not sow corn, but live on milk and flesh, and are clad in skins. All the Britons, indeed, dye themselves with wood which occasions a bluish colour, and thereby have a more terrible appearance in fight.
Caesar's *Gallic Wars*, Vol II

Hidden here, and in the light of all that we have learned up to this point, is the real secret of Caesar's defeat and the Celtic Britons' victory. Knowing what we now know from the deposits analysed on Lindow Man we can say with some confidence that they did indeed *'dye themselves with wood'*. The Romans simply failed to understand the connection between the natural wooded environment of the British Isles and the blue-green copper paint worn by their opponents – green like the woods, green from the earth.

But this is not just any copper paint. This coating spurred them on to death for their sun god, acted as a supreme form of camouflage, and even killed the germs caught in their injuries preventing death by blood poisoning, common among victims of war around three days after even apparently minor injuries.

Imagine the Romans in all their shining and colourful finery, landing unopposed on the beaches, standards high and flags waving, only to find the entire fields and forests coming alive before their very eyes with warriors intent on striking fast, killing many, and fading away just as quickly into the misty oaks and fog filled fern gullies. Two-man chariots raced towards them, the charioteers threw spears and projectiles, even dismounted and exchanged blows, then sped away before the legionaries could gain a sword strike. Later Caesar initiated the development of the 'pilum', a spear with a long slender spike that bent on impact, as Celtic warriors impaled by traditional spears were pulling them out and throwing them back! No wonder the Romans came, saw, and went home again! It was to be a hundred years before they dared to come back.

> We sacrifice unto Mithra, the lord of wide pastures, who has a thousand ears and ten thousand eyes, a God invoked by his own name.
> The Avesta, Sirozah II Verse 16

Rome was indeed the great melting pot of all ancient religions, reaching far beyond the borders of its vast empire, and with various strands rising to prominence under different emperors. All religions had to do was recognise the Roman Emperor as a god (like the Egyptians had before them). Only two religions did not do this – the Druids, political dissidents who never ceased to proclaim uprisings against Roman oppression, and the Christians, religious dissidents who stood fast and worshipped only God. For this reason both religions were equally persecuted and eventually found common ground in Britain and Celtic Europe.

Romans were also worldly-wise sun worshippers who gave us the Cult of Mithras, the worship of 'Sol Invictus' (*Deo Soli Invictae Mithrae!*) the 'Conquering Sun', although the word 'Mitra' meaning 'sun' is first anciently found in the sacred books of Iran and India such as the *Avesta* and *Mishna* where Mithra is created by Ahura Mazda (God of the Zarathushtrians and Supreme Deity of Light to the Persians). Mithra is lower than Ahura Mazda, higher than the visible sun, and creator of the universe as we know it. His birth date has always been the 25th December.

Mithraism also continued worship of the older Greek gods Zeus and Helios and gave us the term 'Magi' (the Biblical 'wise men' of which there were more than three). It also gave us the wider use of the (solar) Christian cross in Europe through the conversion of Emperor Constantine the Great who was only actually baptized a Christian on his deathbed in 337 AD. His cross-monogram 'XP' was based on a vision he had 'in the sun' while preparing for the Battle of the Milvian Bridge, and he heard the words, *'In this sign you shall conquer'*. As a result, many Mithraists were passionately loyal to him. He also won the battle.

The best depiction of Constantine in Britain is the central panel of a mosaic found in the Roman villa at Hinton St Mary in Dorset (and almost always incorrectly identified as the figure of Christ). This 'absorption' of the main beliefs of Mithraism by

Christianity really gathered pace after the full restoration of Christianity from the year 363 AD and the Mithraic religion slowly faded from view over the next few centuries for reasons that are not altogether clear. We will see in a later chapter how and why Christianity absorbed Mithraism and Druidism.

Unusually for a solar cult, Mithraism met and held its rights in purposely constructed chambers below ground 'in the underworld', which have survived all over the Roman world. Its rights included death and resurrection and, as a religion, it particularly appealed to the Roman military who developed their own symbol of power, life, fertility, and bronze, the 'winged phallus' or 'penis with wings' (and sometimes the legs and tail of a lion) which also had a crude meaning in warfare: *'Come and have a go if you think you're hard enough!'* While the male figure of Mithra is almost always shown wearing his distinctive Phrygian cap (later worn by Medieval Masons) he also gives us the first use of a halo derived from the sun-rays previously associated with the Greek Helios.

Commentators who give glimpses into the mystery religion include Ktesias, Xenophon, Duris, Strabo, Pliny, Quintus Curtius, Plutarch, Dion Chrysostom, Statius, and later Christian era writers such as Justin Martyr, Lucian, Tertullian, Dion Cassius, Origen, Jerome and others. Some would say that Mithraism survives still as an underground secret society, or at least its theology does, written into other organisations and creeds.

Romans also produced classical leaf-masks found all over their empire mimicking vine leaves stuck to the faces of Dionysian revellers during the 'Festivals of Bacchus' or 'Fernalia' (24th December) when their old year died and the new year began, and when we now bring trees and foliage from the forest into our houses. Romans also adopted many of the other deities, local, national, and international, who represented the essential procreativity and life force of the natural world found in other societies and today in the Green Man.

Festival of Bacchus parade chariot on a background of grape vines from a Roman feasting hall mosaic in Tunisia

The Solar Copper Cult Develops

3350 BC – Otzi's Cross tattoo represents a healing symbol linked to copper and the sun.

2000 BC – The disc of the setting sun comes to represent a burning copper crucible.

1800 BC – Equal-armed solar wheel crosses start to appear all across Europe.

1700 BC – Wheel crosses appear on Bronze Age burial urns in Britain.

750 BC – European Celts begin extensively using the 'Celtic wheel cross' motif.

55 BC – Julius Caesar invades Britain and encounters blue/green painted warriors.

South American high priest wearing a human skin cloak, jungle god
'Xipe Totec' wearing the face and body skin of a sacrifice victim, and
the Mayan city of Coba covered in jungle in the background

7. Around the World in 80 Decades

At this period in history other cultures were also becoming aware of the qualities of the Green Man and following a remarkably similar pattern to that shown by the Egyptians, Sumerians, Babylonians, and Celts, which is hardly surprising over a period of ancient human development exceeding 8,000 years (80 decades) to the present day.

The Egyptians believed that the world was once covered entirely in water until a mat of reeds appeared and began to grow, forming the living land. Upon this all things were eventually placed by the gods and this became the creation myth of Egypt. Writing was also produced by Egyptian scribes using pens made from reeds and this writing conveyed all things of importance. It is concepts conveyed by writing that moves us to our next civilization, that of the Chinese.

The purpose of words is to convey ideas. When the ideas are grasped, the words are forgotten. Where can I find a man who has forgotten words? He is the one I would like to talk to.
Chinese Philosopher Chang Tzu (Zhuang Zhou) (C.369 BC to 286 BC)

In the Far East the huge and ancient culture of the Chinese also has the 'figure in the leaves'. In China the image of their creator-god is often shown as a man entirely draped in leaves, and the god of medicine and agriculture Shennong is shown wearing clothes of leaves and holding plants with medicinal qualities, medicine being the early science the Chinese are possibly most famous for developing. Even the earliest Quin law (221 BC to 206 BC) concerned itself with the balance of nature, offering protection to birds, animals, fish, and even trees, with wood only being permitted to be cut out of season to make a coffin for a deceased parent.

In addition to this they also had a green stone thought to have similar properties to copper – they had jade. From rulers buried in entire legendary suits made from jade such as the four examples found from 1968 to date in three burials of the Han Dynasty (Western (Former) Han 206 BC to 9 AD/Eastern (Latter) Han 25 AD to 220 AD), to simple eye and mouth patches of jade placed over eyes and tongue in order to prevent decay of the body and escape of the soul, the Chinese put jade to many uses.

Wealth and power in early China were displayed by the possession of jade and bronze vessels. They believed that man had twin souls that parted company at death, one to lie in a tomb and the other to ascend to the heavens (enter the concept of 'heaven'), and both required the sacrifice and offerings of jade. Jade was valued more highly than gold and brought great distances from mines to be worked by metalworkers using abrasive sand. Several kings had jade strung into girdle pendants worn over their robes to make chiming sounds as they walked through their palaces, and there are even surviving accounts of powdered jade being eaten in order to prolong life. Jade vessels often represent the earth and jade discs heaven.

It is a little known fact that a form of green jadeite could be found in Cornwall and parts of the south of England, but was entirely mined out in prehistory to produce rare and beautiful green-stone axes. One wonders how this material may have been regarded by Ancient Britons and Celts?

At the beginning of his reign it is known that Emperor Quin Shihuang (born 259 BC, died 211 BC) worshipped the 'Four Gods', the *'di'* associated with colours, animals, and the elements. Red represented fire, white the tiger, yellow the earth or sun, and blue-green the dragon, which returns us once more to the living life-force that pervades the whole of planet earth (dragons are another story altogether).

Remaining in the Far East, basically the same 'green god' who is the Green Man also appears in Japan. He appears as a protecting spirit in Borneo, Malaysia, and Bali where he is seen in root carvings, in the flowers and leaves above the head of the Buddha, and on temple walls in Tibet and Nepal. He appears as Kirtimukha in the Jain temples of India. In Sanskrit the Green Man is related to the gana Kirtimukha or 'Face of Glory' which is, in turn, related to a lila of Shiva and Rahu. The Face of Glory

A Green Man carved in Bali gazing from swirling sun-rays

is often seen in Vajrayana Buddhist Thanka art and iconography, often incorporated as a cloud form simulacrum or 'recognisable form made from nature' and depicted crowning the 'Wheel of Becoming' or the Bhavachakra. Another god depicted green or as foliage is Amogha-siddhi in Tibet.

The Green Man is in the Middle East, Iraq, Syria and Lebanon; even the mighty Greek and Roman Empires produced classical leaf-masks found all over North Africa, Italy and Europe. The Greeks had Dionysius, or 'Bacchus' to the Romans, and a story to go with him that contains many parallels to other creation and earth myths the world over:

Dionysius was the result of an illicit love affair between the supreme god Zeus and the mortal woman Semele. Unfortunately Semele insisted that Zeus reveal himself in all his splendour as a god and despite Zeus warning that no one would survive witnessing a god in all his glory. Eventually Zeus came down in lightning, fire and splendour, and Semele died as predicted in the ensuing blaze of glory. The result of the love affair was, however, growing in Semele's womb, and Zeus removed the child from Semele's dead body and sewed it into his thigh until he could release it fully developed several months later. Hence the child Dionysius is known to have had two 'mothers' and is often referred to as 'twice-born' going on to become the god of the grape harvest, fertility, ritual madness, religious ecstasy, and the theatre.

In Africa there are many gods and goddesses representing an almost unified but animistic concept of the earth's inherent life-force. These include: Ala, the Igbo goddess of fertility; Asase Ya, the Ashanti earth goddess of fertility who was the wife of Nyame the sky deity who created the universe; Denka, the Dinka god of the sky, rain, and fertility; Mbaba Mwana Waresa, Zulu goddess of fertility, agriculture, rain, the rainbow, and beer; and the Green Man or 'Foliate Head' himself. He actually appears in depictions in the West African Republic of Benin, although it is thought he was taken there by Portuguese missionaries in the 15th and 16th centuries and embraced as a symbol by local craftsmen. In Africa the Green Man/Green Woman distinction is also less clear.

On the American continents other gods depicted green or as foliage are Ayapec the 'all knowing' who appears in Moche ruins of the 1st to 6th century AD on the north coast of Peru, and Tlaloc (pronounced 'Choc'), god of the jungles, in Mexico and South America. The Aztecs and Mayans had a particular slant on the green 'skin' of the earth and, while civilizations north of the equator had bronze and other metals, such civilizations south of the equator relied only on stone and flesh.

At some point in the far distant past a huge meteorite slammed into the earth forming what we now know as the Gulf of Mexico and forcing the sea bed to rise above the waves forming the southern United States, Mexico, the Yukatan Peninsular, and the northern parts of South America. The areas surrounding the edges of the Gulf of Mexico are a honeycomb of dry white limestone rock, which is thin and completely flat. Upon this grows what can only be described as the world's largest 'hedge' that stretches for thousands of miles – but is jungle, entirely comprised of a flat expanse of dense but squat foliage, the tallest trees and bushes all being well under 40 feet/34 metres tall. While still an amazing jungle, this is not the soaring multi-layered growth found elsewhere in the world, but it is the 'skin' that provided every necessity to the survival of the great empires of the Olmecs, Toltecs, Mixtecs, Incas, Aztecs, and Mayans.

These societies have become famous for their temples and ceremonies involving human sacrifice and the cutting out of the beating heart in order to ensure the continued rising of the sun – but what of the green jungle? As already alluded to, they regarded this as 'the skin', which is graphically illustrated by some surviving pottery and painted depictions of their high priests wearing large flayed human skins peeled from their sacrifice victims.

One seated stone sculpture shows the god Xipe Totec wearing the face and body skin of a victim tied at the back, with the god's own living skin painted red and the outer victim's skin painted green.

Another clay figure of a priest shows him wearing a full body cloak made from green speckled mouldy human skin with the arms still attached but rising up from the floor. The point is that the dead human skin gradually changed in the damp jungle environment, from dry dead white flesh to a living mass of green fungus and lichen in exactly the same way as the jungle needed to in order to keep its inhabitants alive.

Many face masks are deliberately decorated green using turquoise stones to represent the resurrecting life-force of the earth, and there are many other similar examples of the inventive use of various green body parts by gods and men. There are literally hundreds of green jade and turquoise masks that have been found in Aztec and Mayan burials over the years, some made from many tiny pieces, and others from solid stone, but all of which appear to serve a similar function to those found in China.

In Mayan legend there was the sun (Tonatiu – 'he who makes the day') and sky (Quetzalcoatl – a wind and storm deity), then the green forest (Tlaloc – god of rain and vegetation), then the white limestone ground (Tepeyollotle – mountain heart and seat of the earth's regenerative power), then the underworld accessible through caves or 'cenote' (Xiutecutli – turquoise lord of fire), the land of the dead (Mictlantecuhtli – lord of death and the underworld).

Sky, wind, fire, earth, rain, water, vegetation, death, and the ancestors produced dozens of lesser deities for which there remains no more space in this small book except to say that they could be common to all ancient societies mentioned thus far, and

A Green Man carved in Bali gazing from roots and swirling sun-rays

common to the identity of the Green Man. Given all the information we now possess regarding archaeology the world over it is the inescapable conclusion that humankind communicated basic physical and religious knowledge over the entire inhabited earth at a period far back in prehistory. There are simply too many specific commonalities – and the concept of the Green Man is certainly one of these.

In another interesting twist we have the famous 'Golden Man' or 'Golden King' of the Aztecs, witnessed by the Spanish Conquistadores during their various invasions after 1519 AD. In this ceremony the ruler was effectively sprayed all over with gold dust to make him shine like the sun in readiness for his religious duties. It was this that fed into the tales of vast repositories of gold hidden in the jungle and the legendary golden city of El-Dorado, thought by the Spanish to be around Lake Guatavita, scene of the Muisca Indians sacred rituals in Columbia. Possibly in Europe powdered copper may have replaced gold as the coating of choice, but with the added twist that the refined shining gold powder would slowly oxidize turning the wearer green as it reacted to sweat as in the case of the Lindow Men and the painted Celtic warriors of Britain.

Powdered gold being sprayed on to the Aztec 'Sun King' as illustrated in a 17th century European manuscript

The physical links here to sun, earth, forest, metal, stone, and human sacrifice, form a graphic illustration of specific beliefs found the world over. Not only do we find beliefs, but we also find the physical culture of copper and copper artefacts of almost identical types at around the same times from the distant lands of China, right across the land masses of the globe, to the cultures of North America. And finally bringing us up to date...

In Islam Khidr, al-Khidr, or Abul Abbas Ahmad al Khidr, 'the Green One' (also sometimes transcribed as Khidar, Khizr, Khyzer, and Khizar) is a revered figure who the Qur'an describes as a *'righteous servant of God'* who possesses great wisdom or mystic knowledge. He is most often said to be a contemporary of Moses (C.1500 BC), but in other variations of his story he lived further back in time at the same time as Abraham (C.2000 BC), the mythological Persian king Afridun and Nashiya bin Amus. The 18th sura *The Cave* presents a narrative where Khidr accompanies Moses and tests him about his oath to not ask any questions.

Tom Cheetham (a modern day authority on Islamic mysticism) identifies the Khidr of esoteric Sufism with the Green Man. In his book about the work of Henry Corbin and others, concerning the 12th century Muslim saint Ibn Arabi he develops the idea of the Green Man/Khidr as the principle mediating between the imaginary realm and the physical world.

On a similar theme, author on spirituality and architecture William Anderson writes:

There are legends of him (Khidr) in which, like Osiris, he is dismembered and reborn; and prophecies connecting him, like the Green Man, with the end of time. His name means the Green One or Verdant One, he is the voice of inspiration to the aspirant and committed artist. He can come as a white light or the gleam on a blade of grass, but more often as an inner mood. The sign of his presence is the ability to work or experience with tireless enthusiasm beyond one's normal capacities. In this there may be a link across cultures...one reason for the enthusiasm of the medieval sculptors for the Green Man may be that he was the source of every inspiration.

In recent times certain strands of Islam seem to have embraced a very destructive and violent view of human sacrifice but would do well to remember the words of the Prophet, as it is written: *'The ink of the scholar is more sacred than the blood of the martyr.'* (Muhammad C.570 AD to 632 AD).

Islamic star and cross motifs from a Medieval merchant's house in Souse, Tunisia

'The Fires of the Otherworlds' by Anthony Potts

8. Handling Stolen Gods – The Birth of Christianity

And he took the blind man by the hand, and led him out of the village; and when he had spit on his eyes and laid his hands upon him, he asked him, 'Do you see anything?' And he looked up and said, 'I see men; but they look like trees, walking.' Then again he laid his hands upon his eyes; and he looked intently and was restored, and saw everything clearly. And he sent him away to his home, saying 'Do not even enter the village.'
Yeshua's conversation with a blind man in the Revised Standard Version Bible, New Testament book of Mark, Chapter 8 verses 23-26

A fool sees not the same tree that a wise man sees.
William Blake – *The Marriage of Heaven and Hell*, Proverbs of Hell, C.1793.

Not many people realise that 'The Church' has never really existed as one coherent unit at any point in its entire history! At the point we today consider to be the beginning it was no exception. It grew from the cultures of prehistory; Sumeria, Egypt, Babylon, Canaan, Greece and Rome, and it flowed into the Hebrew and Jewish movements of the 'Holy Land', which survive today.

Broadly speaking the religious movement which began in the days of Yeshua ('Jesus' so named to avoid confusion with 'Joshua') immediately adapted itself into three distinct zones, each adopting a huge and inevitable corpus of existing religious material from the geographic regions in which it was based.

Yeshua (Jesus) lived from between 7 BC-6 BC to around 36 AD, based on modern calendar dates, and created what we can confidently call the Middle Eastern Church, which continued the already well established Biblical tendency to adopt material originally found in Egypt and elsewhere in the Middle East. The frequent argument that Yeshua is simply 'a composite of all the Egyptian, Greek, Jewish and Roman gods and traditions present in Israel at the time of his birth' may appear a valid criticism, but the argument that any divine creator would send a messiah to fit every religion is equally valid, rendering the point irrelevant. Inevitably the religious capitol of this newly emerging branch of religion became Jerusalem. Then, somewhere at some time, a Roman insulted a follower of 'The Christ' and the term *'Christian'* was born.

Almost immediately the new religion left its Middle Eastern base and crossed the Mediterranean, ultimately arriving in Europe and Britain, in particular at the legendary hands of Joseph of Arimathea, his band of disciples, and other apostles fleeing persecution in the Middle East between 36 AD and 54 AD. In actuality this established the Celtic Church as the oldest Church in the world to be founded outside Jerusalem itself and which is a universally recognised state of affairs to this day. Consequently the adoption of expedient suitable material continued with this new branch of the Church adopting Celtic and Druidic material and most likely establishing its religious capital in the centre of the British Isles around Chester, the Wirral and North Wales.

Cross and victor's wreath from a 4th century Romano-Christian mosaic

Disciple Peter and the convert Paul also played an integral part in the spread of Christianity into Europe with the final conclusion that they were made into saints by the branch of the Church that adopted Rome itself as headquarters, the final known resting place of the body of Peter. In the continuing trend for adopting established religious identity this branch of the Church chose a Roman and Mithraic identity, which blossomed out into the Roman Catholic (or 'universal') Church, which claims its foundation date as 60 AD and adopted a great deal of existing Roman religious material such as Mithraism.

So why is this important?

The key to this adoption strategy explains how and why the

entire pre-Christian Celtic and Druidic religion became absorbed into Christianity in what we see now as such an obvious way, including the person and concepts of the Green Man – not something anyone would directly associate in any way with Christianity!

Recent etymological (language based) research by the University of Wales into the meaning of the names of Celtic gods and goddesses has shown that one Celtic deity, Viridios, has a name essentially meaning 'Green Man' in the Celtic languages and in Latin. This would be a good candidate for the character absorbed into the church. Broadly speaking the newly emerging church needed a concept easily understood by the cultures of the day – Greeks, Romans, Celts and Druids – and the Green Man embodies blood sacrifice, life force, death, regeneration and resurrection, a creator god, and one with a very long prehistoric pedigree indeed.

If further proof of this were needed we can turn to the visit of the Roman Catholic Saint Augustine to Kent in 597 AD to 601 AD to convert the Saxons. Astonishingly these religious missionaries became the first on record to discover their faith already being practised by the household of the king to whom they bore their message! We know that Ethelbert's wife, Queen Bertha, was a Christian and already had a Frankish (French) Christian chaplain named Liudhard. Having arrived and sized up the situation Saint Augustine then wrote to Pope Gregory:

In the Western confines of Britain there is a certain royal Island of large extent, surrounded by water, abounding in all the beauties of nature and necessaries of life [probably the 'island' of Wirral or North Wales]. *In it the first Neophytes of Catholic Law, God hath beforehand acquainted them, found a church constructed by no human art, but by Divine construction by the hands of Christ Himself, for the salvation of His people. The Almighty has made it manifest by many miracles and mysterious visitations that He*

continues to watch over it as sacred to Himself, and to Mary, the
Mother of God.

Translated from the *Epistolae ad Gregoniam Papam*

Pope Gregory the Great then replied with some surprising advice, which follows that given by the 4th century BC philosopher Plato in his *Republic*:

Destroy as few pagan temples as possible; only destroy their idols, sprinkle them with holy water, build alters and put relics in the buildings, so that, if the temples have been well built, you are simply changing their purpose, which was the cult of demons, in order to make a place where from henceforth the true God will be worshipped. Thus the people, seeing that their places of worship have not been destroyed, will forget their errors and, having attained knowledge of the true God, will come to worship him in the very places where their ancestors assembled. In former times they used to sacrifice a large number of cattle in honour of demons; there is no need to change their customs at festivals. Thus, on the feast of dedication or on the feasts of martyred saints whose relics have been placed in the church, they should build booths out of branches round the church as they used to round pagan temples, and celebrate the festivals with religious banquets... You do not climb a mountain in leaps and bounds, but by taking it slowly.

From Gregory the Great, Letters XI, 56

Plato wrote to the effect that settlers in a new country should first discover the shrines and sacred places of the local deities and reconsecrate them to the corresponding principles in the colonists' own religion, with festivals instituted on the appropriate days, and that there should be at least 365 festivals in the course of the year. This was an almost universal practice in antiquity. As we have seen, the Green Man is found everywhere almost certainly as a result of following this principle, or something similar to it.

In one statement we have the explanation why churches are located where they are with respect to ancient sites, and why Medieval foundations could later justifiably lay claim to the sites, relics, and customs of former religions. Thus the Green Man developed so far that he became the Green Christ, the Green Bacchus of Wine, the Green Lion of Judah (often illustrated like a cat and symbol of Christ's royal blood-line), eventually even as the Green Knight.

Cross from the side of an early Christian 4th century baptismal pool discovered in North Africa

**Norman Green Man on an outside door at Kilpeck Church,
Herefordshire**

9. Trying to See the Wood for the Trees – Verderers and the Church

I cannot find anything better in man than that he know, and nothing worse than that he be ignorant
Saxon King Alfred the Great (849 AD to 899 AD)

Initially blame for the actual image of a carved face peering through leaves appearing in Europe rests predominantly with the Vikings and their stone-building descendants the Normans. This does not, however, rule out the influence of the Celts, Saxons, Danes, Picts, Welsh, Irish, and other occupants of Britain and Europe who must certainly have retained a strong memory of the myth behind the Green Man, but it is in the stone carvings of the Norman invasion period that we find our first surviving true Green Man church carvings here in Britain.

Some of the best survivals can be found in the churches of the Romanesque period, which pre-dates Gothic and approximately straddles the end of the Saxon period and the start of the Viking. It was the Saxons who probably supplied the local masons who carved them and, in the first part of the Norman period, the Norman and Viking noble society that commissioned and paid for them. Fine examples in the UK can be found at Kilpeck in

Herefordshire and Leominster in Shropshire, but there are thousands more right across the British Isles and Europe.

And then there is also a need that each should understand where he came from and what he is – and what will become of him.
Wulfstan, Saxon Archbishop of York (1002 AD to 1023 AD)

In one statement Wulfstan, the 11th century Saxon Archbishop of York, captures perfectly the purpose of the Green Man appearing in church architecture. For thousands of years the British Isles were covered with a thick canopy of trees, so much so that it was said you could release a squirrel on the south coast and that it could reach the northernmost islands of Scotland without ever having touched the ground. So it remained throughout the early, middle, and late Medieval periods before deforestation of these islands.

The first part of the human race to attempt to impose its will upon the forest on a large scale was undoubtedly the Romans who perceived the close proximity of woodland as a threat to their safety – and for very good reasons already outlined. They even had a set distance enshrined into their regulations of clearance either side of main roads they constructed in order to

prevent ambush. But a huge woodland useful to humankind does not manage itself.

At some point around the time the Romans withdrew from the British Isles a new category of woodland carers came into being known to history as the 'Foresters'. It is thought that these uniquely skilled and competent farmers of the forest first became confederated into an official career path during the upheavals of the Saxon period when it would have been a dangerous oversight on the part of regional rulers to allow the vast resources the forests on offer to go to waste. It is said that King Athelstan (924 AD to 940 AD) was the Saxon king responsible for establishing the first guilds and the Foresters would undoubtedly have been one of these. Instead of individuals working small parts of the forests piecemeal, large sections became a working industry managed by the Foresters Guild certainly by the 10th century AD.

These men were known as *Verderers, Verdigers*, the *'Men of Vert'*, (*'Vert'* being the Norman-French word for 'Green'), the men of *Verdigris*, which is the bright blue-green substance produced by oxidized copper, or in English 'Green Men', quite literally as the production of the green cloth their clothing was made from involved dying material using ascetic acid (human pee) and copper to produce a permanent verdigris-based green dye. They quite literally wore a 'skin of green'. Considering all that has passed in this book to this point it will come as no surprise that the entire mythology of the Green Man should eventually pass into the care and use of Foresters.

By Norman times the guild symbol of the Foresters had clearly become the Foliate Head and, as such, they had the right for it to appear in their places of meeting and worship – taverns and churches. Other guilds did the same resulting in images of boots and shoes, various tools, animals, plants and fish, depictions of occupations and pastimes, and a whole collection of other weird symbolism finding its way into churches.

Forest chapels all over the country began to develop containing lots of Green Men and the pubs and hostelries frequented by the 'Men of the Woods' started to be named The Green Man, Foresters Arms, Royal Oak, etc. These patterns can still be identified in church buildings and old taverns, positioned to take account of the huge royal hunting forests of the Medieval period.

If such forests had their own unique laws – which they did – then why not their own unique and appropriate forms of myth, ceremony and religion?

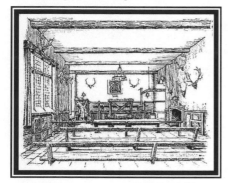

A Victorian illustration of 'The Court of Verderers' in the New Forest, Hampshire

It is these Foresters and Forest Guilds that are ultimately responsible for the material we find associated with Sir Gawain and the Green Knight, Robin Hood, Jack in the Green, Herne the Hunter, and the Old Man of the Woods so favoured by later writers. In essence this is the birth of a unique branch of folklore known as 'wood-lore'.

But many of these 'forest nobles' were not content with simply being woodsmen. Many, like Robin Hood, aspired to rise up the social ladder and become knights. Whereas the Knights Hospitaller specialised in all things medicinal, it was the famous and renowned Knights Templar who were to become the undisputed custodians of all things mysterious, mystical, and religiously ancient.

There is absolutely no doubt that the Knights Templar and Knights Hospitaller were a product of their times. They developed directly out of the ages that had passed before them, warrior monks like the post-Roman 'Culdees', holy men and

Druidic Celtic Christians, who travelled the roads of Britain and the continent spreading their own particular brand of Druidic-Christian spirituality, wearing long woollen cloaks, travelling in threes, carrying swords, and adopting the strongest trends of expedient religious belief widely accepted at the time. These were ancient yet fervent exponents of the Celtic Church. The result is that we also find the 'cult of the head' widely accepted from prehistory right into the Viking Age, absorbed into their religious beliefs and surviving iconography.

Celtic Druidic-Christian Holy Men or Culdees from a stone found at Housesteads Roman fort on Hadrian's Wall on the Scottish borders

From the Old Testament beheading of Goliath by the future King David (C.1040 BC to 970 BC), to the New Testament beheading of John the Baptist by Herod Antipas the Tetrarch (C.20 BC to 40 AD) at the wish of Salome, his wife Herodias' daughter, we see the ancient belief that the sum total of the human being (the soul) resides in the head, seat of the senses, intellect, reason, and through which we see, hear, and communicate with the world around us. This is the true mystery of the famous Celtic stone heads and only in very recent times do we point to the heart when referring to our soul. The ancients saw the heart merely as the seat of the emotions. It appears that if you had the head of your enemy then you quite literally owned them and they could not pass on to the underworld and the after-life.

In nations such as Norway, Scandinavia, Denmark, Germany, Iceland, and Viking England, those who have studied the mythology of the Norse peoples feel that depictions of the Green Man could have been inspired by deities such as Freyr or Odin as both have many attributes found later associated with the Green Men found throughout Early Medieval Europe. Also back in Mesopotamia we first encounter the distinctive depictions of the Tree of Life, which more than likely lent its identity to the one found in Jewish mysticism and the Kabala – and then possibly to the one found in Viking Norse mythology:

This tree is known as the 'World Tree', an ash named Yggdrasil linking the three worlds of Viking mythology and upon which Odin hung to receive the runes. One root reached into Asgard under which was the well of Urd (fate) where the gods held council every day, one root delved into Jotunheim and sheltered the well of Mimir, the repository of wisdom where Odin left his eye in exchange for a knowledge giving drink, and the final root stretched into Niflheim and sheltered the spring of Hvergelmir, source of all rivers that contributed to the creation of the world.

In life and as living human beings our past is the roots of the tree, our present existence is the trunk looming large and obvious to us, and our future is the branches reaching into time and space, infinite in number yet discernible as larger and small pathways trapped within a limited shape. We are indeed *'as trees walking'* and the Vikings applied this further to the whole of creation and the world.

The Norse god Freyr, Lord of Fertility, also warrants closer examination as there are elements common to the Green Man myth the world over, which are found in his surviving legend. Freyr and his sister Freyja were extremely beautiful and immensely powerful. As the radiant and bountiful god of sunshine and increase, Freyr was considered the most glorious of the gods and was often placed on the same level as Odin and Thor such that in the great temple at Uppsala his statue stood alongside those of Odin and Thor, although the specific forms of Freyr's worship have been lost. The contents of this book probably point towards the details of his worship. As an exception to this is that peace and fertility appear to have been closely linked in the minds of the Vikings and the fertility gods had special responsibility for keeping the population free from strife and warfare. Because Freyr was considered a god of peace it is known that weapons and bloodshed were banned in his temples.

Adam of Bremen, an 11th century AD German chronicler, was scandalized to report that the Uppsala idol had a 'huge phallus' symbolising Freyr's role as god of human procreation and male potency. As for the practices attending his worship, the chronicler merely stated that they were too obscene even to describe. Another similar writer named Saxo also commented disapprovingly of Freyr's worship as he found the gestures of the priests effeminate and unmanly, and he too declined to describe what he saw in any further detail. We do, however, have some surviving legends:

Freyr owned two particular treasures. One was the ship 'Skidbladnir' given to him by the dwarves, which was said always to attract a fair wind when launched. Although it was large enough to hold all the gods fully armed, it was so skilfully constructed that it could be folded up and kept in a pouch. Freyr's other magical possession was the golden boar 'Gullinbursti' ('golden bristles') which could travel through the air faster than any horse could gallop, and whose brilliant metallic lustre lit up the darkest nights.

In Celtic mythology the boar was a symbol of the forest, strength in a fight and, it also appears, a sun symbol frequently made of bronze. However, Freyr was particularly associated with horses, which both archaeology and the written sagas suggest were dedicated in sacrifice to him. *Hrafnkel's Saga* relates how Hrafnkel, known as Freysgodi ('Priest of Freyr'), loved no god more than Freyr and shared all his most valuable possessions with him. He had a magnificent stallion of which he was particularly fond, which he called Freyfaxi ('Mane of Fryer') and dedicated to the god. According to the saga Hrafnkel vowed that he would kill anyone who rode upon the horse. When someone eventually did it was his own unwitting shepherd and the story details the consequences of the killing when Hrafnkel felt he had to honour his word, the details of the ensuing revenge, and the inevitable battles that followed.

Another story about the Christian King Olaf Tryggvason tells how he set out to destroy the temple of Freyr at 'Thrandheim', the modern Trondheim, in Norway. There he came upon a stud of horses said to belong to Freyr, which were kept to be killed in ritual ceremonies and offered as food to the god. Olaf showed his contempt for Freyr by mounting the only stallion in the stud while his men mounted the mares, and together they rode to the temple to destroy the god's statue.

The Swedes trace the ancestry of their kings to Freyr, and their ruling house was known as the 'Ynglingar' after 'Yngvri', which is an alternative name for the god in that country. According to a tale in Snorri's *Heimskringla* the gods had once lived and ruled on earth. When Freyr had been king of the Swedes for a time, peace, harmony and affluence came upon the land. When he passed away news of his death was suppressed by his attendants who secretly placed his body in a mound and paid tributes of gold,

Norman Green Man/Sheila-Na-Gig in Melbourne Parish Church, Derbyshire, showing a clear Viking design influence

silver and copper to him for three years in order to maintain peace and prosperity. After three years the community eventually discovered the truth, but they were so convinced that offerings had kept their land free from strife that they continued to venerate him. In this tale we can once again see connections to gods, death, the underground realms, metals, offerings and fertility of the land.

It is known that the powerful and respected Sami shamans of the Norse lands surrounding the Arctic Circle practised their animistic beliefs from the Middle Ages, before the rise of the Vikings, right into the 18th century AD, and most likely influenced the Viking world view. To them the whole of creation were their gods, but they also had one god that specifically cared for all forest animals named Laib Olmai, possibly the last surviving remnant of the prehistoric cult that gave us Herne the Hunter.

We would do well to remember that the last Icelandic Viking sagas were only written down in the 1460s AD and that the Sami nation still survives today as the oldest continuous prehistoric tribal nation in Europe.

'The Face in the Oak Leaves' by Anthony Potts

10. Custodians of the Ancient Mysteries Arise

A man is a fool who undertakes a journey only to view his own face.
From the Crusading Journal of Duke Roger of Lunel,
September 1096 AD

It was in November 1095 AD that Pope Urban II called for a Crusade at the Council of Clermont and every conceivable type of warrior signed up on the understanding that their immortal souls would automatically make it into their particular view of heaven through this venture. By the summer of 1099 AD the 1st Crusade had reached Jerusalem with more Vikings, Danes, European mercenaries, and ordinary folk from every country in tow than noble knights! Some of the mercenaries on Crusade were even Moslems!

They took Jerusalem on the 15th July 1099 AD and Godfrey of Bouillon, Duke of Lower Loraine, formed the Knights of St John to tend to injured knights when the city was finally secured. The following year in 1100 AD Godfrey died and Baldwin I succeeded him as King of Jerusalem. By 1113 AD the Independent Order of the Hospital of St John in Jerusalem (or Knights Hospitaller) was confirmed by Pope Paschal II and run under Augustinian monastic rule.

In the space of less than twenty years the Middle East had

become a seething melting pot of every conceivable European, Mediterranean, North African, and Middle Eastern culture in a swirling pool of human knowledge and creativity that ultimately gave birth to the huge developments that became known to history as the Renaissance. If it wasn't for the information exchange brought about by Medieval Crusades we may never have had Leonardo Da Vinci! Possibly the greatest culture shock in all this was all the material that the Crusaders had in common with their opponents, rather than the differences, and one of these common themes was the Green Man. When weapons were laid aside (as they often were) and the language barriers bridged by the realisation that the whole world still spoke Latin, the orders of knights became custodians of their new secrets through the teachings and discoveries of the East.

In 1114 AD the Bishop of Chartres in France referred to another forming military order called the Militia of Christ, who it is now generally thought became the Poor Knights of the Temple of Solomon (or Knights Templar) in 1118 AD, formed by Hugues de Payens and Godfrey de St Omer to protect the increasing number of pilgrims then to be found on the road from Jaffa to Jerusalem. In that same year King Baldwin I died to be replaced by Baldwin II and there is no doubt that many communications between popes, kings, knights and monks had led to the creation of the Templars. However, just nine knights were not going to pose much of a threat to the combined forces of Islam, leading modern day commentators to question the many real reasons why the Templars formed the way they did.

> *It seems that a new knighthood has recently appeared on the earth.*
> *It ceaselessly wages a twofold war both against flesh and blood, and*
> *against a spiritual army of evil in the heavens.*
> *'In Praise of the New Knighthood' (De Laude Novae Militiae)* by St
> Bernard of Clairvaux written C.1130 AD)

As conflicts continued the Knights Hospitaller followed the Templars in becoming a fully military order once again in 1123 AD, and in 1124 AD Hugues de Payens officially became the first Grand Master of the Templars. This led him to undertake a European 'tour' and he visited Britain in 1127 AD to rally support, during which he crucially recruited the French St Bernard, Abbot of Clairvaux, the foremost writer in Medieval Europe at that time on matters of the female aspects of God and an authority on anciently absorbed traditions. By this time the order of Templars was fully monastic, initially Augustinian in rule like the Hospitallers before it, but later changing to Cistercian.

Mysteriously in 1128 AD the Templars were still recorded as being only nine knights and a few recruits, famously having only one horse between two knights – hence this image appearing on their seals as a sign of poverty and brotherly support. In 1130 AD St Bernard completed his seminal work *In Praise of the New Knighthood* and Pope Innocent II was finally persuaded to confirm and accept the Templars in 1139 AD.

What commenced then was the famous order that became hugely rich through gifts, grants, inheritance, and the invention of the travellers cheque (or safe exchange of money by written pledge for a small fee). There are far too many mysteries attached to the Templars and Hospitallers to go into further detail here, but suffice to say that the result of their beliefs and obvious connections to Forester knights all over Britain and Europe, the little detached face in the leaves became a fully accepted, indeed essential, feature in every Templar church, Romanesque, Gothic, or High Gothic, constructed from that time foreword.

The concept of the 'Green Christ', which is the head ('soul') of Christ spewing living foliage (the 'blood of salvation') to bring eternal life and resurrection to the viewer, came into being during this period, as did many of the Green Lions, Green Cats, etc. which have the same basic meaning. Some of the more demonic Green Men may allude to the darker side of nature and humankind, and some depicted with horns may echo early representations of Moses with the 'divine horns' or 'twin flames' of God upon his head, or Alexander the Great and the 'horns of Amun' – Amun Ra, supreme sun god of the Egyptians (and later adopted by the Greeks). In past times horns were not necessarily a bad thing.

In 1146 AD the 2nd Crusade began and the Templars adopted their distinctive Cross Pattee, or 'equal-armed cross', which is an unashamed declaration of the beliefs outlined in this book and nothing whatsoever to do with the cross of Christianity. Time spent in the Middle East was now casting its influence.

As time progressed, the Templars produced myriad variations on this theme and included a cross shaft and Calvary steps on their tombstones and depictions, giving the illusion that the cross was a Christian one while closer examination shows it clearly not to be. Even the shaft was often co-opted into another form such as foliage, a tree, a plant stem, a spear pinning a beast at the foot of the gravestone, etc.

Green Men also appear on these tombstones, usually at the foot end spewing foliage out in the traditional manner, and representing a prayer for resurrection, just like the extremely fine 13th century AD example found at Norton Priory in Cheshire, England, shown here.

Green Man spewing oak foliage from the foot of a 12th century tombstone at Norton Priory, Cheshire, which develops into an equal-armed 'rose cross' design

Some tombs show a circle containing the 'Tau' cross in the shape of the letter 'T' instead of a full wheel cross. This represented the Medieval view of the world, that it was divided into Asia in the whole top half of the divided circle, Europa in the lower left hand quarter, and Africa in the lower right hand quarter, with Jerusalem at the centre of the circle where all three zones met. Evidently the knights so buried were well-travelled men of the world.

On the 2nd October 1187 AD the famous Islamic warrior ala ad-Din Yusuf ibn Ayyub, or in Kurdish 'Saladin', re-captured

Jerusalem and, despite the famous 3rd Crusade featuring King Richard 'Coeur-de-Lion' in 1189 AD, continued to hold it up to his death in 1193 AD.

There are then many more Crusades, the 4th Crusade (1202 AD), which included many children, the 5th Crusade (1218 AD), followed by 6th (1228 AD), 7th (1239 AD), 8th (1240 AD) – none of them successful. Then, in 1244 AD Jerusalem, was lost back to the Turks. The 9th Crusade was undertaken in 1248 AD, followed by the 10th (1271 AD), both fail until, in 1291 AD, the Holy Land was finally entirely lost to the Saracens and no strongholds were held by any European Crusaders. The Templars were by then the richest religious order in history, they had the largest navy and the world's first permanent standing army, but they were essentially out of a job.

The end of the order was then a swift decline.

On Friday 13th October 1307 AD King Phillipe IV 'The Fair' of France ordered the arrest of all Templars – although someone had clearly tipped them off as their navy departed France the evening before and very few knights remained in their preceptories to be arrested. On the 22nd March 1312 AD a Papal Hearing officially dissolved the Knights Templar and instructed that all property should transfer to the Knights Hospitaller, much to the annoyance of King Phillipe who wanted to seize it all for himself.

On the 18th March 1314 AD the last Grand Master Jacques de Molay and Geoffroi de Charnay Preceptor of Normandy were roasted to death in a firepit on an island in the River Seine in Paris and famously swore with their dying breaths to see the Pope and King at God's judgment before the end of the year. Amazingly both King and Pope died before the year ended. Recently discovered Vatican documents show that Pope Clement V actually absolved the Templars of all wrong-doing. However, on the 20th April Clement died, followed on the 29th November by the then ruling King Philip IV 'according to the Templar curse'.

Meanwhile, back in Britain, the first three King Edwards actually favoured the Knights Templar and gave them ample time to re-locate to Wales, Ireland and Scotland, and to hand over their property to the Knights Hospitaller. It is now almost certain that Templars appeared at the battle of Bannockburn in Scotland fighting for Robert the Bruce in 1314 AD, in 1319 AD the newly formed 'Knights of Christ' became recognised as an order, and it was 1334 AD before King Edward III finally dissolved the Templars in England. In response the King then formed The Knights of the Round Table and The Most Noble Order of the Garter by 1348 AD. Continuity of Templar and Hospitaller traditions and beliefs is hardly surprising under these conditions.

A couple of testaments to the Templars, Foresters, knights, monks, and their belief systems, survive to torment us and defy perfect interpretation. One is the bizarre tale we now know as 'Sir Gawain and the Green Knight', written in parchment; the other is Rosslyn Chapel, Midlothian, Scotland, begun in 1446 AD as a weird testament written in stone. One thing is for certain, the Green Man plays the most prominent role in both.

Victorian engraving of the interior of the 15th century Lady Chapel belonging to the St Clair family who built Rosslyn Chapel, in Scotland

11. The Green Man Rides In – Forest Chapels and the 'Golden Thread'

The fire that ravaged the famous Cottonian Library in 1731 AD fortunately spared a small and undistinguished-looking manuscript of the late 14th century. Now safely housed in the British Library, this unique manuscript preserves probably the best book of Medieval romance in English Literature, *Sir Gawain and the Green Knight*.

The manuscript is written in a superb poetic version of a dialect that belongs to the mid north-west area of England and includes a large number of words that hark back as far as the Viking Age. This is a place where the modern counties of Cheshire, Staffordshire, and Derbyshire meet, a place where many of the locations in which the story is set still exist almost as they did when the manuscript was written, and a place where the Arthurian legends as a whole were, in reality, first born.

Remembering all the connections that have passed previously in this book, and bearing in mind that it was most probably set in writing by a monk or royal scribe who obviously knew more than they could possibly admit, the tale runs like this:

It is Old Christmas Day in mid January and the annual celebrations are well under way in Arthur's court when the door bursts open and a green man dressed as a green knight on a green horse rides in demanding that the most worthy knight face him in a New Year challenge of faithfulness to Arthur. The challenger must cut off the Green Knight's head with the knight's axe in a single blow, but the Green Knight will return the blow for every test the knight fails over the next year and a day. No one moves!

Gawain slowly rises and draws the axe towards him watched in silence by the Green Knight who slowly bows his head in front of Guinevere. Gawain strikes the blow. The Green Knight then picks up the head, places it back on his shoulders, looks wryly at Gawain and says: 'See you in a year and a day at the Green Chapel. Mark well your tests this year fair knight.' Then he mounts up and rides out.

Gawain sets off from Arthur's court at Holywell in North Wales and crosses to the Wirral where he encounters early Viking and Saxon settlers ('Trolls') who challenge him to many fights, which he wins. He then reaches the River Mersey and rides down the southern bank until he reaches a fortress in a forest. This turns out to be the home of Bercilack, owner of the castle fortress and surrounding forest (and therefore a 'Forester Knight'), *who introduces Gawain to his wife and housekeeper. Bercilack desires to get to know Gawain a little better, but he is in the midst of the hunting season and will be away during the day for the next few days. He suggests that Gawain remains his guest during this time and he will surrender all that he captures each day for the next three days if Gawain will stay and do the same.*

The following day Gawain awakes and, as his eyes clear, he realises that he can see the silhouette of a woman. It is Bercilack's wife, without her veil, who drifts slowly towards him and makes a mild attempt to seduce him with her words. He declines to leave his bed and she eventually kisses him quickly on the cheek and leaves. As night falls Bercilack rides in carrying a magnificent deer, which he presents to Gawain who has nothing to give him, but a swift kiss on the cheek.

When Gawain wakes the next day he looks carefully for Bercilack's wife, but she is not in his room. Relieved he arises and begins to dress. Suddenly hands slide about his waist and she again tries to seduce him, whispering tenderly in his ear. With incredible restraint Gawain chooses not to turn round and she is forced to kiss him on the ear before she leaves. Bercilack returns from the hunt that evening with a huge wild boar and all that Gawain has for him is a kiss on the ear.

This time Gawain is woken by the outline figure of the lady sitting astride his bed, and she tries to seduce him again by pointing out that this is his final chance. After the usual persuasive exchange of seduction and Gawain's attempts to refuse without offending his host's fair lady, she seems to weaken in her resolve to conquer him. She makes one last request for a final kiss on the lips, climbs off the bed and allows Gawain to rise and dress. As he does she moves behind him and adds a green sash under his surcoat. Later that day Bercilack returns having caught only a fox and Gawain greets him, but claims to have caught nothing that day.

Next day Sir Gawain rises and finds his room and the castle deserted, he has to open the great doors himself and lead his own horse out. He rides through the forest, which eventually brings him to the Green Chapel (thought to be Lludchurch, in Staffordshire). *He dismounts at the path that leads down into the mossy green rock chasm below and descends the steps where he encounters the imposing figure of the Green Knight, waiting axe in hand. Gawain moves forward to a rock upon which he slowly places his head. It is the day after Old Christmas Day.*

The Green Knight raises his giant axe, which slams down onto the edge of the rock. Gawain flinches and remembers the gentle kiss of Sir Bercilack's wife on his cheek. Raising the axe again the blow is repeated on target, but this time the axe stops within an inch of Gawain's neck as if the Green Knight is just taking aim. This time Gawain remembers the breath of Sir Bercilack's wife on his neck and the kiss on his ear. The axe is raised for a third time and the blow catches the side of Gawain's neck. Gawain jumps up drawing his sword and claiming that blood flows and justice has been done, just in time to see the figure of the Green Knight change into the laughing Bercilack.

Bercilack explains that the whole adventure was a test for Arthur's 'most noble knight'. Had Gawain taken advantage of Bercilack's wife he would also have betrayed Arthur, his king, and failed the moral test. He only failed by not declaring the green sash, which he had been given for passing the test, and the cut on his neck was the result. Had he failed completely he would have died. Gawain rides back to Arthur's court where his tale is told and Arthur declares that all the most worthy knights of his court should wear copies of the green sash from that time forward.

Hidden somewhere in this tale could be the ritual through which those already in the Foresters Guild or connected to the Knights Templar could initiate a new member. A challenge over a set period of a year and a day, service and protection of a queen and king, the time of year through which three tests of chastity and loyalty were to be performed, the literal or symbolic penalty for failure, the wearing of a green sash, and a clear connection to knighthood.

Can we take this further as a coded definition of a 'Golden Thread' woven through thousands of years of human history? Yes, I believe we can.

Two categories of individual appear to be always present throughout the history of the Green Man: prehistoric copper workers and representatives of the Divine, heroes and priests, warriors and Druids, Forester Knights and monks.

Hand in hand this path is one of 'the initiated' and 'the Divine', the representatives of the practical arts of the land combining with those who knew what religious practices and conventions were required in order to continue living in the right way. Although not unique to the Green Man, this Golden Thread of secret knowledge can still clearly be identified in later historic buildings and theology. Villard de Honnecourt, the 13th century master mason who kept a notebook, refers to the face that forms into leaves as the *'tete de feuilles'* or 'Head of Leaves', and this is the only known record so far discovered of the name given to the Green Man in Medieval times.

Modern copper sculpted 'Tete de Feuilles' on the sundial at Norton Priory, in Cheshire

One amazing structure, a testament in stone, produced by master masons in Late Medieval times, from the 15th and 16th century AD, survives in Scotland; Rosslyn Chapel, in the sleepy Scottish village of Rosslyn seven miles south of Edinburgh.

Consider the lilies of the field, how they grow; they neither toil nor

spin; yet I tell you, even Solomon in all his glory was not arrayed like one of these. But if God so clothes the grass of the field, which today is alive and tomorrow is thrown into the oven, will he not much more clothe you, O men of little faith?
The words of Yeshua in the Revised Standard Version Bible, Matthew's Gospel, Chapter 6 verses 28 to 30

The Collegiate Chapel of St Matthew at Rosslyn would not have been unique in any way before King Henry VIII dissolved the monasteries across Britain in 1536 AD and the Parliamentarian troops of Oliver Cromwell repeated the exercise of destruction a hundred years later during the English Civil War between 1642 AD and 1650 AD. Buildings were smashed, libraries burned, and religious idols destroyed.

Such chapels, churches, cathedrals and monasteries as Rosslyn once existed all over the British Isles, but most now exist either as ruins or were rebuilt in later ages, sometimes with no consideration whatsoever to their past. Also destroyed and dispersed were the great libraries of these foundations, which would, without doubt, have shed a great deal of light on the many mysteries with which we are now struggling. Many times in history has secret esoteric knowledge been forbidden and destroyed by those with another religious or political agenda. This little book hopes to reconstruct and present one of those lost threads.

Enshrined in the almost perfect stonework of Rosslyn Chapel is the mystery known by Foresters and Knights at the time the chapel was first conceived by William Sinclair. He was a Templar who died in Spain in 1330 AD while attempting to escort the heart of Robert the Bruce to the Holy Land. Although continental Templars were outlawed and arrested by King Philip of France in 1307 AD and moved out of England by 1334 AD, they remained for a time longer in Scotland as is clearly shown by the many surviving burial monuments showing continuity into the 13th,

14th, and even 15th centuries.

The present standing structure of Rosslyn Chapel owes its foundation to the year 1446 AD and had taken on its present form with the addition of houses and gardens by 1523 AD. Despite the fact that the full vision for the church was never realised, what we have contains countless depictions of the Green Man – the guide books say more than a hundred – including a 'primary face' staring out of protruding foliage directly above the St Clair family altar in the small private rear Lady Chapel. Out of four altars in this tiny chapel, this is the one that sits on the main axis of the building, directly behind the high altar in the main body of the church, so it is that this little Green Man defines the main east-west axis of the entire building. This is the axis of life rising in the east and eventually passing to the 'lands of the dead' below the horizon in the west.

It is likely that the chapel was also originally painted in colour, as Medieval foundations once were, and it would be a real experience to leave the literal surrounding forests and woodland to enter a mystical and spiritual 'woodland' containing Gothic columns as trees, arches forming branches, and populated by myriad mystical and religious signs and symbols peering out including Green Men. Virtually a Druid Grove in stone filled with hidden mysteries.

While no genuine mystical records pertaining to the early Knights Templar have yet been found, we have seen that it is still possible to reconstruct at least one aspect unique to the Forester Knights using buildings and surviving legends, picking out the ancient Golden Thread that was and is the Green Man.

Can we truly call this thread 'Gold'? Yes we can; the gold is the copper as it melts in the crucible, the colour of the all-mighty sun as it rises in the east and sets in the west, then to rise resurrected again in the east, and this is the reason why quite a number of the 'Green Men' are actually painted in shining gold.

The unfinished and mysterious Rosslyn Chapel in the tiny village of Rosslyn, in Scotland

The Solar Copper Cult Slowly Dies

1080 – Verderers are appointed by the Saxons and Norman barons as Foresters.

1118 – Formation of the Knights Templar and Knights Hospitaller.

1200 – The rise of Robin Hood legends, Jack-in-the-Green, King Arthur, etc.

1300 – High point of Gothic Architecture includes many Green Men.

1400 – Many Forest chapels such as Rosslyn develop (although few now survive intact).

1500 – Shakespeare and others enshrine folklore into published material.

Medieval 'rose cross' coffin lid of Hugo Bissop, Knight, Weobley, in Herefordshire

12. Printing Killed the Mythological Star

Antiquities are history defaced, or some remnants of a history that have casually escaped the shipwreck of time.
Writer and commentator Francis Bacon (1561 AD to 1626 AD)

The various periods of time we have chosen to bring together to form the Early, Mid, and Late Medieval, did not suddenly come to an end with the birth of Henry VIII in 1491 AD or his coronation in 1509 AD. The tales, rituals, festivals, orders and habits of the ordinary inhabitant of the British Isles continued very much as they always had.

Modernisation under the Tudors brought the bronze metal of ancient prehistoric weapons into the manufacture of better guns and cannons that still killed people. These strange links between copper, war and death continued but, just as the 'creative reed' of the Egyptian scribe had written sacred text, so now copper plates developed with the arrival of the Age of Printing. The magic simply transformed and developed once again.

The Age of Printing brought together surviving stories and presented them to a wider audience. Modernisation and reform followed the modern pattern of re-invention and re-branding. This can clearly be seen in the emerging literature of the 15th and 16th centuries.

Although Julius Caesar lived in the 1st century BC, Arthur and his knights lived at the turn of the 6th century AD, Macbeth in the middle of the 11th century AD, and Robin Hood for the large part in the 12th century AD, it didn't stop writers such as Sir Thomas Malory (*Morte d' Arthur*), Edmund Spencer (*The Faerie Queene*), and good old William Shakespeare from converting surviving tales into live performances and ultimately best sellers.

Mythical characters and creatures tumble in cascades alongside historical personages through the pages of such works as *A Midsummer Night's Dream, Twelfth Night, Cymbeline, Othello,* etc. In his early prose work *Spring and All*, William Carlos Williams gave high praise to Shakespeare's ability to collect stories when he said that Shakespeare is *'the greatest university of all'*, although Shakespeare's 'history' has not always proven to be right!

If anything this proves that the ordinary man still retained a consciousness of these popular tales through continuing festivals and monuments from the past. In a masque by Thomas Nashe, *Summer's Last Will and Testament,* composed in 1592 AD and printed in 1600 AD, after the exit of *'Satyrs and wood-Nymphs,'* the character commenting upon the action remarks: *'The rest of the green men have reasonable voices...'* which is almost certainly the first ever use of what was to become the modern term for our pursuit in this book.

However, despite this literary hint towards the future, out of this slowly building landslide of printed literature the Green Man as we know him thus far did not survive.

Instead the legends and rituals of this most ancient of religions became swallowed up by the huge wave of printed works of every kind and topic that flooded out of the 16th and 17th centuries. The printed work was subject to higher control, editing and oversight by royal and religious establishment from the word go.

After the English Civil War the Church clearly had the upper hand when it came to popular religious writing with Geoffrey Chaucer (*The Canterbury Tales*), William Langland (*Piers Plowman*), the *King James Bible* released with the king's approval in 1611 AD and now widely available in a form that the general public could read, followed by writers such as John Milton (*Paradise Lost* and *Paradise Regained)* and John Bunyan (*Pilgrim's Progress*). A new form of 'Churchianity' was being born, one that turned for inspiration to town living, industry, enlightenment, science, and the absolute domination of humankind over the natural environment. It chose to turn its back on its ancient roots. No place for the Green Man!

Inspired mystic writer, artist and Gnostic William Blake (1757 AD to 1827 AD) mysteriously combined many of the elements found as I have written them in this book to produce his strange work *A Memorable Fancy* in about 1793 AD, which perfectly captures the 'Hell' that the printing house had become:

I was in a Printing house in Hell & saw the method in which knowledge is transmitted from generation to generation.

In the first chamber was a Dragon-Man, clearing away the rubbish from a cave's mouth: within, a number of Dragons were hollowing the cave.

In the second chamber was a Viper folding round the rock & the cave, and the others adorning it with gold silver and precious stones.

In the third chamber was an Eagle with wings and feathers of air: he caused the inside of the cave to be infinite: around were numbers of Eagle like men, who built palaces in the immense cliffs.

In the fourth chamber were Lions of flaming fire, raging around & melting the metals into living fluids.

In the fifth chamber were Unnam'd forms, which cast the metals into the expanse.

There they were reiev'd by Men who occupied the sixth chamber, and took the forms of books & were arranged in libraries.

William Blake, *The Marriage of Heaven and Hell – A Memorable Fancy* C.1793 AD.

'The Man of Leaves' by Anthony Potts

13. Leading the Parade – Jack-in-the-Green

*There are only two powers in the world, the sword and the pen; and
in the end the former is always conquered by the latter.*
Napoleon Bonaparte (1769 AD to 1821 AD).

Do we have any evidence that the Green Man faded away as the
Industrial Age began? Yes – in many ways we do.

A very good friend of mine once passed on the advice he had
been given which has proven to be very true: *'Always look for what
isn't there!'* Sometimes we get so preoccupied searching for what
we can see, the important character or piece of information slips
quietly out of the back door without us even noticing and we are
left completely unaware that a vital something is missing. So it is
with the Green Man after the start of the English Civil War and
victory by the Puritan Parliamentarians between 1642 AD and
1650 AD.

Despite the revival of 'ancient' orders such as Druids,
Freemasons, Witchcraft, Rosicrucians, and the Order of
Foresters, the Green Man and his entire religion simply fades
back into the forest from whence he anciently came, never to
appear in the writings of any of the newly rising orders! That's
not to say the principles were lost, humankind simply had a
change of heart and turned away from the essential survival
strategy of living in harmony with the green world, and chose
instead the path of human self-survival through domination,
science and industry. There was simply no place for a demanding
nature god in the rising world of modern civilization – so they
simply left him out.

Wrought iron ornament from Hampton Court 1690

But all was not lost. After all, this awesome ancient power covered the whole face of the earth, took power from the eternal sun, and encompassed the universal male energy of regeneration essential to the survival of all things, leaving a legacy behind as old as humankind itself. Humankind's use for the Green Man may have ended, but his continuation was assured through the very thing over which he had sway – the creative arts.

Illustrations of the Green Man in all his forms did not stop being produced, in fact their popularity in iconography increased as manufacturing and mass production gradually took over, ironically almost in pace with the fading away of his real meaning. His popularity with the ordinary folk also changed into new forms such as that found in the 18th century prints of chimney-sweeps, May Day Jack-in-the-Greens found in London and other parts of the British Isles and, with the arrival of the traditional Victorian Christmas, the Holly King, characters covered in garments made from seasonal leaves.

Jack-in-the-Green became established as the traditional English May Day cone of foliage constructed over a frame carried by a participant (often a chimney sweep) in the Victorian May festivities. This idea first appears when the Victorians developed and expanded the idea of May Day garlands from the 16th and 17th century, principally created for maypoles then extended to other forms. Popular folklore writer Sir James Frazer mentions the tradition in his seminal work *The Golden Bough.*

It is thought to have begun in London, but one of the best surviving examples of Jack-in-the-Green today leads the Knutsford Royal May Day procession in the village of Knutsford, Cheshire, on the first Saturday in May, at an event first begun in 1864 AD.

Victorian transfer printed ceramic showing a dancing Jack-in-the-Green

The maypole is, of course, a very late and thinly veiled representation of a Tree of Life and the festivities revolve around spring fertility and the mating of the male and female, anciently done for real, but done symbolically from the days of the prudish Victorians, otherwise Queen Victoria would not have been amused.

Following on the heels of the Victorian view of Jack-in-the-Green are the early 20th century fantasy writers such as J.R.R.

Tolkien (1892 AD to 1973 AD) and C.S. Lewis (1898 AD to 1963 AD) both of whom made wide use of characters inspired by the forest and fertility deities of the past. Tolkien seems to focus his interest in earth and forest spirits into characters in the world of *The Hobbit* and *Lord of the Rings* such as the 'man of the forest' Tom Bombadil, Goldberry the 'Daughter of the River', Old Man Willow, the forest Wizard Radagast the Brown, Barrow-wights, and of course the forest Ents or living tree spirits.

In contrast C.S. Lewis takes a more traditional approach using Greek and Roman characters combined with those from Germanic, British and Irish fairy tales. In *The Chronicles of Narnia* he has Santa Claus putting in an appearance, Mr Tumnus the Faun and Puddleglum the Marsh Wiggle as principle characters, and many other of the Narnian creatures created by Aslan the Lion are obviously connected to the Green Man legends and forms of the past – although neither writer appears to have a firm grasp of this.

Other prominent fiction and fantasy writers of the period are so far removed from the principle material or 'Golden Thread' of the Green Man that they do not warrant a detailed mention. Firm connections in their material beyond coincidence or a simplistic popular view can not be found. Occasionally it is a different story in the development of religion.

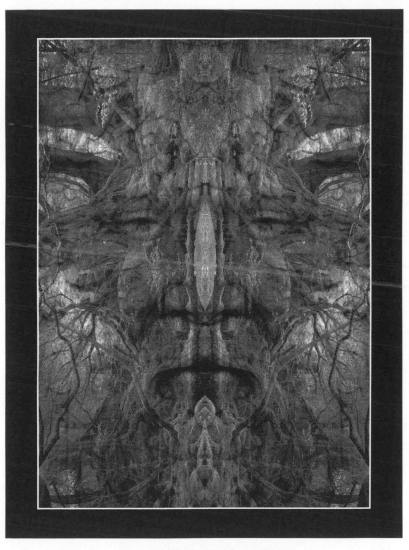

'Tree Spirit' by Anthony Potts

14. Fifty Shades of Green

'Know me better man.'
The Ghost of Christmas Present (Holly King) in *A Christmas Carol* by Charles Dickens, published in 1843 AD.

It is a widely held fact that the Victorians and the British Empire brought to light possibly the largest combined library of human knowledge since the famous Library at Alexandria almost two thousand years before. As a result huge amounts of folklore, fact, history and archaeology were combined and recombined to produce the paths, religions, societies and orders of the 19th and 20th centuries. Of these orders that embraced European folklore, probably the most relevant strand to grow into modern times is that of Witchcraft and Wicca.

Broadly speaking it is understood that the herbalists, wise women, village midwives, pellars, woodsmen, naturists and folklorists of the 18th and 19th centuries were progressively brought together and into the public realm by writers and figure-heads including Gerald Gardner (1884 AD to 1964 AD), Alex Sanders (1926 AD to 1988 AD), Aleister Crowley (1875 AD to 1947 AD). They combed the writings of the past, added material from

Druids, magicians, and Freemasons, to create a new united craft that could genuinely claim to have ancient roots. Witchcraft in all its forms has an ancient pedigree, but it is the relatively recent version that concerns us here.

In modern Witchcraft we have the Wheel of the Year, an eight-spoke sun wheel, which represents the turning of the earth and sun to create the European planetary year divided into eight significant festivals: four major festivals including two solstices, and four minor 'quarter days'. This wheel is often depicted as the eight-spoke Babylonian Star of Ishtar, which takes us back to the solar cross where we began. At its oldest root the original beginning of traditional Witchcraft resides with the ancient Cult of Ishtar – a mystery seldom revealed.

The modern established festivals are: midwinter (Yule) major solstice, Imbolc (spring), Ostara (Easter) major vernal equinox, Beltane (first day of summer), Litha (midsummer) major solstice, Lughnasadh (Lammas), Mabon (Harvest Home) major autumn equinox, Samhain (Halloween), and then back to midwinter.

Overall the concept is simple; the god rises to power at midsummer, after which he declines. The goddess gives birth to her fruits in the autumn, and rises to power at midwinter, after which she declines. As the god rises again he mates with the goddess in the spring (May Day) after which she continues to decline until she gives birth. This is the European 'year myth' that has existed as long as time itself, the goddess in all her various forms is the earth, the god in all his various forms is the Green Man, and the driving impulse is that of sex.

Through the 20th and 21st centuries we have seen the development of a more popular and acceptable strand of Witchcraft called Wicca, which has become widespread in the United States. Other strands have developed, such as Cornish and Irish, and it can be said that England, Wales, and Scotland all have their own variations. While Witchcraft became legal to practise again after the repeal of the Witchcraft Act in 1952 AD, it can also be said that most traditional Witch covens have remained entirely or partially closed and hidden, while the Wiccan covens have essentially gone public. No doubt somewhere in this process still lurks the Green Man – even if practitioners don't always know who or what he really is!

**Green King image from below a choir stall in Southwell Minster,
Ludlow, Shropshire**

Modern depictions and mask of the Green Man from the Witchcraft
Museum, Boscastle, Cornwall

15. Mystic Rhythms – It's a 'Green' World Now

My young men shall never work. Men who can not dream, and wisdom comes to us in dreams. You ask me to plough the ground. Shall I take a knife and tear my mother's breast? Then when I die she will not take me to her bosom to rest. You ask me to dig for stone. Shall I dig under her skin for her bones? Then when I die I can not enter her body to be born again. You ask me to cut grass and make hay and sell it and be rich like white men. But how dare I cut off my mother's hair?

The words of American Indian Wanapum dreamer-prophet 'Smohalla' C.1815 AD to 1895 AD)

Before modern civilisation set in, the earth was regarded as the one universal deity, not just the material earth, but the spirit by virtue of which, according to the ancient philosophers, it is living creature; usually female because it 'receives' the power of the sun and is animated and made fertile by it. Today we often call this 'living earth' the 'Gaia Principle' after Gaia the Greek mother-goddess of the earth. The products of this union produced by nature can be said to be male as they constitute the surface body of the earth which, like the body of all mankind (humankind) is corruptible and subject to change. In science the biology of the entire planet is interrelated and essential for its continued survival. This remains a fair summary of the modern view of nature. The 16th century alchemist Basilius Valentinus set the basis for this view when he wrote:

The earth is not a dead body, but is inhabited by a spirit that is its life and soul. All created things, minerals included, draw their strength from the earth spirit. This spirit is life, it is nourished by the stars, and it gives nourishment to all living things it shelters in its womb. Through the spirit received from on high, the earth hatches the minerals in her womb as the mother her unborn child.

That 'mineral child' included copper, the child's identity is that of the Green Man, his mother is the earth, and his father is the sun.

13th century 'Green Bacchus' from panelling in Daresbury village church, Cheshire, birth place of Lewis Carroll

Another mystic thread finds a conclusion with us here in the modern age. During the mid 18th century German units of infantry foot soldiers began to dress in green and other forest colours in order to blend in when required to take on sniper duties against their enemies. Over time this developed into the camouflage we know today, which has created, in effect, the same 'green warriors' encountered by Julius Caesar two thousand years ago. Ironically a great many modern firearms use ammunition that fire copper-jacketed bullets making copper still a warrior's choice for the kill.

No one in ages past would have known the subject of this book as the 'Green Man'!

Lady Raglan is responsible for first using the term 'Green Man' in an article she wrote in 1939 AD entitled 'The Green Man in Architecture' for publication in *The Folklore Journal* and the name has stuck in modern times ever since.

Man thinks of himself as a creator instead of a user and this delusion is robbing him, not only of his natural heritage, but perhaps of his future.
Helen Mary Hoover, 20th century American children's author

Modern day commentators have found aspects of the Green Man in figures such as the Old Testament Biblical prophet Elijah and the Muslim prophet of eternal life Khidr. Further aspects have been associated with European Celtic deities such as Cernunnos and Sylvanus, and more recent folklore figures such as Derg Corra, George-a-Green (Green George), John Barleycorn, Robin Goodfellow, Puck, and it has also been suggested that the story of Robin Hood was born from the same mythology – which is not strictly true as I believe he also existed as a real person in the 12th century. Robin is a good example of the way in which later writers and publishers combined legendary material to disguise, rubbish, and play down earlier information no longer taken seriously. A more modern embodiment of the 'Spirit of the Forest' and of eternal life and youth is found in Peter Pan, who enters the modern Victorian world from Neverland clothed in green leaves.

As we have seen based on the seasonality of ancient rites and rituals, even Father Christmas (Santa Claus) is often shown swathed in ivy or dressed in green, cream and brown in early depictions suggesting connections to some kind of woodland spirit, perhaps even the ancient Herne the Hunter through the influence of the Sami shaman.

In reality these are turning wheels which have no end. Of course these characters have commonality when broken down to their essence. But the Green Man remains the Green Man because he has a claim to be the oldest and most firmly established – a now hidden concept unchanged by time, culture, and location.

In modern systems of belief the Green Man has been reduced to an interesting collection of leafy faces that can be purchased at craft fairs and shops selling New Age, mystical and Witchcraft items, and hung around the house and garden to promote aspects of natural growth and fertility.

If only the purchaser knew the dark reality contained in these pages!

Green Man over the doorway of a timber-framed Tudor manor house in Claverley, Herefordshire

Human sacrifice, beheading and the 'triple death', symbol of warrior, war, death, passing over and the Celtic afterlife, provider of sunshine but also of metal – green, gold and red – earth, foliage, and life-blood – birth, death, resurrection – secret symbol of Druid, Knight and Medieval Mason, bringer of the chaos of wine, consort of the spring, keeper of the forest where no man dwells, inspiration of writer, playwright and poet, Humbaba, Osiris, Shennong, Viridios, Tete de Feuilles, the Green Man – but above all very much unique and ever-present whether we accept and acknowledge him or not.

So what about that 'old time religion' – can we piece together the basic structure and beliefs that once surrounded the Cult of the Green Man? Yes we can.

Is this cult different in any way to simple animistic fertility cults found the world over? Yes I believe it is, and a great deal more developed and complicated.

A) The Supreme Deity=the sun, shown as a disc, circle, the circular mouth of a burning crucible filled with molten copper or gold, and also represented by circular metal jewellery such as round broaches, neck torques, or torque bracelets. Sometimes red like blood.

B) Symbolically the equal-armed cross can also be combined to form the solar wheel cross, which has been used to represent various religions down the centuries, but usually the sun, earth, or later resurrection as a concept. This also feeds into the tree as an image representing life created by the sun (the vertical), and the earth upon which the sun acts and into which the dead are placed (the horizontal). It is from the action of the sun (shown in Egyptian Amarna Dynasty illustrations as many rays terminating in hands) that all things originate.

C) The earth=female giving birth to all things, the sun=male providing fertilising life. This sets the first equation in motion in the minds of the ancients: *The damp earth turns green when the sun is hot – copper comes from the earth and is green when found and mined – once melted copper turns gold – the sun is gold and glows like the opening in a crucible – therefore copper comes from the sun – and so do green plants.*

D) Copper, gold, and other metals (from the earth and melted by fire) are suitable offerings to both earth and sun (usually personified as gods), frequently as a wish for resurrection or as an important gift for the after-life. This also includes the various warrior cults that have been associated with metal in the past and their formula goes something like this: *A warrior deals in life and death – weapons deal in life and death – warriors, human sacrifices and divine rulers can be coated in metal as they are involved in life and death – gods and goddesses can be metal as they deal in life and death – divine rulers and emperors can utilise metal as they have the power of life and death.*

Such items and persons as this are suitable candidates to be sent to the 'otherworld' or 'next life', which is not up, but down into the earth from which everything originates. There are suitable 'doorways' into the earth such as caves, pools, rivers, dug or built monuments below ground, or through fire (cremation), or ritual destruction of people or objects ('ritual death'). We also have the formula: *Copper is the blood of the earth – when melted it oxidizes and turns red – blood tastes very much like copper on the tongue – copper weapons cut and release blood – weapons are the property of warriors – warriors rule over life and death.*

In ancient times there was always a priesthood somewhere keeping these formulas alive and this led into knowledge sustained by the various orders who combined the roles of priesthood and warrior, reaching its heyday in the Medieval periods. With the advent of the printed word this knowledge became so secret, controversial, and unpopular that it all-but died out or became over-popularised and trivialised in the extreme.

Green Man carved on a pew in St Bartholomew's Church, Tong, Staffordshire

Where would I like the Green Man to return if he were to return today?

As our world continues to spiral into technological chaos, the Green Man should be the quintessential symbol for all those who support and defend the natural aspects of the planet and wish to see man's worldwide planetary destruction stop. Active and militant not passive and undefined. Remember the anonymous saying: *'Today everything is possible, yesterday has gone.'*

Symbolically the Green Man is saying: 'Either we stop poisoning and destroying or, one day, he will rise up and destroy us!' The ancients understood this. No one takes on the power and might of the natural world and wins.

What is apparent from writing this book is that the gradual decline and loss of the true meaning of the Green Man brought in a new period in human existence that was no longer based on the overall harmony of a universally recognised world ecology and balance. Humankind developed the ability to cause damage that the planet (or 'Green Man' force) could no longer easily repair. We call it 'pollution'. The ancients would have said that if the planet can repair what we do, then we can do it (as they did). However, if the planet can not repair what we do (such as some heavy industry, chemical pollution, atmosphere depletion, oil extraction, fracking, animal and plant extinction, nuclear and atomic power, deforestation, etc.) then we should leave these things alone and move on. How our attitude has changed from that of our ancestors. Their message to us today would be: 'Just because we can, doesn't mean that we should.'

While it may be argued that humankind had no environmentalists in the past, the reply would be that they had no need of them. This subject clearly shows that religion played that part for millennia and this little book hopefully restores the position of concern for our environment to the religious arena now there is a clear and demonstrable religious path to follow once again. There definitely is an ancient and very long-standing tradition of religion of all kinds fighting for the survival of the planet. It's not just politics!

Overall humankind has lived in relative harmony with the environment, but we have seen unprecedented destructive acts all over the planet in just the past couple of centuries. If we continue to forget the Green Man then he will also forget us. Either we grow to understand and appreciate what the Green

Man symbolises as countless millennia of our ancestors have, or this book will, one day, have no one left to read it.

For many millennia we used to sacrifice ourselves to save the planet, now in modern times we appear to be trying to sacrifice the planet to save ourselves. Impossible. Instead we should be re-founding this lost religion.

Three Great Truths

'Hear me, my brother,' he said. 'There are three great truths which are absolute, and which cannot be lost, but yet may remain silent for lack of speech.

'The soul of man is immortal, and its future is the future of a thing whose growth and splendour has no limit.

'The principle which gives life dwells in us and without us, is undying and eternally beneficent, is not heard or seen, or smelt, but is perceived by the man who desires perception.

'Each man is his own absolute lawgiver, the dispenser of glory or gloom to himself; the decreer of his life, his reward, his punishment.

'These truths, which are as great as is life itself, are as simple as the simplest mind of man. Feed the hungry with them.'

From *The Idyll of the White Lotus* by Mabel Collins, Published in 1890 AD

Picture Credits for Chapter Heading Designs

Introduction and Terminology: Modern day depiction of the Green Man face adapted by Mark Olly from a Victorian engraving.

1. **Herne and Horns:** Illustrative reconstruction of a prehistoric cave painting of a hunter dressed in animal skins and horns from a cave at Trois Freres, Ariege, France.

2. **The Watchman of the Forest Never Sleeps:** Ancient Persian depiction of the 'Star of Ishtar' from the reverse of a pendant.

3. **The Man in the Ice and the Man in the Chalk:** Coptic cross pendant of C. 300 AD based on prehistoric European, Mediterranean and North African rock carvings.

4. **Egypt – A Matter of Life and Death:** The 'All-Seeing Eye' of God adapted from the Egyptian Eye of Horus shown here from a 16th century Hermetic manuscript.

5. **Beyond Dark Waters:** Leafy Green Man face drawn from a detached fragment of Medieval carving.

6. **The Face of the God – We Came, We Saw, We Went Home Again:** 2nd century Roman Bronze Cross thought to be from a horse harness of some kind and found at Housteads Fort on Hadrian's Wall.

7. **Around the World in 80 Decades:** A detailed 19th century Victorian engraving of the ancient Chinese 'Creator God' draped in leaves.

8. **Handling Stolen Gods – The Birth of Christianity:** Modern graphic illustration of the Tree of Life depicted as an oak by Mark Olly.

9. **Trying To See the Wood for the Trees – Verderers and the Church:** A group of four 14th century Late Medieval Foresters and their dogs illustrated by Mark Olly.

10. **Custodians of the Ancient Mysteries Arise:** Carved stone

111

modern adaptation of the classic Templar Cross from a Masonic grave.

11. **The Green Man Rides In – Forest Chapels and the 'Golden Thread':** Chubby face of a Rosslyn Chapel Green Man found over the St Clair family altar in the Lady Chapel – and now available to hang on the wall as a souvenir.

12. **Printing Killed the Mythological Star:** Green King illustration adapted from an 18th century book print.

13. **Leading The Parade – Jack-in-the-Green:** Foliate Face adapted from a wood carving on the front drawer of a classic Victorian mirror-back side board C.1880 AD.

14. **Fifty Shades of Green:** The first known full depiction of the Wheel of the Year created in a full colour manuscript by Hildegard of Bergen C.1098-1179 AD.

15. **Mystic Rhythms – It's a 'Green' World Now:** Modern day concrete panel of the Green Man face peering through sage in a garden.

Two Green Men on the underside of a choir stall seat in Southwell Minster, Ludlow, Staffordshire

Moon Books invites you to begin or deepen your encounter with Paganism, in all its rich, creative, flourishing forms.

If you have enjoyed this book, why not tell other readers by posting a review on your preferred booksite. Recent bestsellers from Moon Books are:

Journey to the Dark Goddess

How to Return to Your Soul

Jane Meredith

Discover the powerful secrets of the Dark Goddess and transform your depression, grief and pain into healing and integration.

Paperback: 978-1-84694-677-6

ebook: 978-1-78099-223-5

Shamanic Reiki

Expanded Ways of Working with Universal Life Force Energy

Llyn Roberts, Robert Levy

Shamanism and Reiki are each powerful ways of healing; together, their power multiplies. *Shamanic Reiki* introduces techniques to help healers and Reiki practitioners tap ancient healing wisdom.

Paperback: 978-1-84694-037-8

ebook: 978-1-84694-650-9

Pagan Portals – The Awen Alone

Walking the Path of the Solitary Druid

Joanna van der Hoeven

An introductory guide for the solitary Druid, *The Awen Alone* will accompany you as you explore and seek out your own place within the natural world.

Paperback: 978-1-78279-547-6

ebook: 978-1-78279-546-9

A Kitchen Witch's World of Magical Herbs & Plants
Rachel Patterson
A journey into the magical world of herbs and plants, filled
with magical uses, folklore, history and practical magic. By
popular writer, blogger and kitchen witch, Tansy Firedragon.
Paperback: 978-1-78279-621-3
ebook: 978-1-78279-620-6

Medicine for the Soul
The Complete Book of Shamanic Healing
Ross Heaven
All you will ever need to know about shamanic healing and
how to become your own shaman...
Paperback: 978-1-78099-419-2
ebook: 978-1-78099-420-8

Shaman Pathways – The Druid Shaman
Exploring the Celtic Otherworld
Danu Forest
A practical guide to Celtic shamanism with exercises and
techniques as well as traditional lore for exploring the Celtic
Otherworld.
Paperback: 978-1-78099-615-8
ebook: 978-1-78099-616-5

Traditional Witchcraft for the Woods and Forests
A Witch's Guide to the Woodland with Guided Meditations and
Pathworking
Melusine Draco
A Witch's guide to walking alone in the woods, with guided
meditations and pathworking.
Paperback: 978-1-84694-803-9
ebook: 978-1-84694-804-6

Wild Earth, Wild Soul
A Manual for an Ecstatic Culture
Bill Pfeiffer
Imagine a nature-based culture so alive and so connected,
spreading like wildfire. This book is the first flame...
Paperback: 978-1-78099-187-0
ebook: 978-1-78099-188-7

Naming the Goddess
Trevor Greenfield
Naming the Goddess is written by more than 80 adherents and
scholars of the Goddess and Goddess Spirituality.
Paperback: 978-1-78279-476-9
ebook: 978-1-78279-475-2

Shapeshifting into Higher Consciousness
Heal and Transform Yourself and our World with Ancient and
Modern Shamanic Methods
Llyn Roberts
Ancient and modern methods that you can use every day
to transform yourself and make a positive difference in the
world.
Paperback: 978-1-84694-843-5
ebook: 978-1-84694-844-2

Find more titles and sign up to our readers' newsletter at http://www.johnhuntpublishing.com/paganism. Follow us on Facebook at https://www.facebook.com/MoonBooks and Twitter at https://twitter.com/MoonBooksJHP. Most titles are published in paperback and as an ebook. Paperbacks are available in physical bookshops. Both print and ebook editions are available online. Readers of ebooks can click on the live links in the titles to order.